sound tragically unjust to one who for six months, during some of the hardest fighting of the war, lived with an Irish regiment and buried its dead. Surely, however justified as a whole may be that condemnation of the Irish we so often express, we should still remember to give honour to those Irish soldiers who lived a credit to their nation, and who died, like their English comrades, in the One great Cause.

LILLE, *November* 1918.

CONTENTS

From Cloister to Camp

FROM CLOISTER TO CAMP

President Poincaré arriving at the gates of Lille on his first visit after the liberation of the city, showing the Guard of Honour from the 1st Royal Munster Fusiliers, 21st Oct, 1918.

[Frontispiece.

FROM
CLOISTER TO CAMP

BEING REMINISCENCES OF A PRIEST
IN FRANCE, 1915 TO 1918

BY
FR. DOMINIC DEVAS, O.F.M.

Author of "A Modern Franciscan"

WITH FRONTISPIECE AND MAPS

SANDS & CO.
LONDON: 15 KING STREET, COVENT GARDEN
EDINBURGH: 37 GEORGE STREET

1919

TO

ELIZABETH

WHOSE FATHER FELL AT SERRE

13TH NOVEMBER 1916

FOREWORD

THESE pages are a simple personal record of my experiences of war in France. They lay no claim to be history, and yet neither are they romance, but simply the gathering together of the abiding impressions of one whose part in the war was infinitesimal, but for whom the war itself was the daily and all-pervading factor in life during three and a half years.

Of my work as a priest, to say all is impossible and so I say little. It was always day by day, but more especially towards the end, the continuous setting in which my life ran, profoundly influencing myself personally and—one longs to hope—not without some helping influence for those with whom my days were spent.

Neither do I mention, except rarely, the inestimable friends I made amongst men and officers. To know them was a real privilege, and to live with them a real pleasure. Their memory at least remains with me as a sacred possession, for in all too many cases their death came to me as an irreparable loss.

Part II. may perhaps be allowed to have a significance of its own. The remarks one hears made by Englishmen on the part the Irish took in the war

PART I

CHAPTER I

EARLY DAYS

FOR me the war began on a certain Saturday night about 11 P.M., 8th May 1915, when I jumped hastily into an empty second-class railway carriage in Rouen station and started away up the line almost immediately, leaving my valise behind me.

We—there were two other chaplains with me—had arrived at Rouen that morning. We had gone as instructed to see Father, now Bishop Keatinge, and I had learnt from him that I was to be attached to the 1/1 South Midland Field Ambulance in the South Midland Division He told me there was no hurry to leave, and that I had much better wait until the next day. Inquiries at the station, however, led to the discovery that if I did not leave that night I should have to wait till Monday; and so, in my first enthusiasm, I decided to go at once, confidently anticipating I should arrive somewhere next morning where I could either hear or say Mass.

After having carefully noted the position of the station, possessed myself of the necessary papers from the R.T.O.'s [1] Office, and reassured myself as to the time my train left, we went to an hotel for dinner.

[1] Railway Transport Officer.

Leaving early—I was determined to be in time—we reached the station again at about 9.30. It was now that my first troubles began. Leaving my valise and the bag containing my Altar Set, I began to inquire as to where exactly my train was to start from. I had of course visions of its starting at least by or near a platform. No one I asked seemed able to give me the slightest information, and I was quite ignorant of the right way of setting about to get it. At length in despair, seeing a likely looking troop train due to start about eleven, I took up my stand there in the hopes that the information I had sought in vain would in due course be brought to me. The minutes sped by. It was getting near eleven now when suddenly—I really forget how—I discovered my train was elsewhere. My two companions, who had come to see me off, kindly promised to follow me with my luggage, whilst I rushed on ahead to secure a seat. After interminable wanderings over endless tracks of line I arrived at my train at last, only to be thrust into my carriage by an infuriated R.T.O., who declared I should have reported an hour ago, and was absolutely indifferent to my anxious inquiries as to the fate of my luggage. My two companions I had long since lost in the darkness, and my one ray of hope lay in the kindly words of a soldier on the railway staff who assured me my possessions would be sent on by the next train. I did not see them again for a fortnight, and that I retrieved them at all was due to the kind exertions of the two chaplains who had wisely decided to wait till Monday.

And so now here was I in an ill-lit railway carriage alone with my thoughts, which were none too cheery,

and with all my luggage reduced now to the contents
of my haversack I did the only obvious thing and
lay down to sleep. I must have slept fairly well for
dawn was just breaking when I finally awoke. I had
nothing to eat and no one to talk to, and the train
crawled slowly on as though, like me, it had only
the vaguest idea of its destination. At one point I
noticed some camp fires burning under the shelter of
a little ridge, and I wondered vaguely if perhaps we
were approaching the battle zone and whether the
enemy lay beyond; but the train still pushed on in
lazy unconcern. As soon as it grew light enough I
said all my Office for the day. When that was
finished I resumed once more my vigil at the
window. Nothing seemed to break the eternal
monotony of that awful journey. The sun rose
higher and higher. At two o'clock I said Matins
and Lauds for the following day. Then I remembered I had a book with me, a pocket edition of
Admonition by John Ayscough. I brought it out
from my haversack and read it straight through from
cover to cover, but my mind wandered constantly to
the grim realities of the present, and I have no recollection now what the book was about. Once, when
the train was indulging in one of its frequent and
protracted halts, I got out in desperation and asked
an officer, whom I saw in the next compartment, if he
had anything to eat. He was unsympathetic, and
merely murmured something about having nothing
but his " Iron Rations,"[1] a term which was quite un-
intelligible to me at the time. I could but get into

[1] Emergency rations of tinned beef and bicsuits, tea, and
sugar which every soldier is supposed to carry.

my seat again as the train moved off, and hungry,
lonely, and disconsolate, wait for what the future
might bring forth. I remember, after leaving Calais
I think, looking out of the window and seeing the
line in front of me descending gradually into a vast
plain, which seemed to my ungeographical mind to
extend into the very centre of Europe.

At length, about five o'clock that Sunday evening,
we reached Bailleul, and everybody seemed to be
getting out. Accordingly I got out and made my
way to an aged and harassed R.T.O., to whom I
showed the " movement order " I had been given at
Rouen. The R.T.O.—it surprised me then but does
so no longer—was positively rude. He wanted to
know if I had any idea where I was going, or what
I had come to Bailleul for. Of course I hadn't.
Finally it transpired that a bus of some kind was in
due course to leave for Steenwerck, which apparently
was on my way. My next and pressing business was
food. I had tasted nothing since dinner the night
before at Rouen. Not knowing Bailleul in the least
—and from the station it did not show many possi-
bilities—I made for the first estaminet I saw and got
an omelette and some ham in the back room. When
I had finished I had a forlorn look for my luggage,
hoping against hope it might have been thrust at the
last moment into a coach at the end of the train.
There was, however, no sign of it, and I resigned
myself then to waiting patiently for the bus.

The scene at the station was not without interest
to one of my little experience. The troop train I
had come up in had barely disgorged its shouting,
cheering masses of men—Wiltshires mostly, I re-

member, and one wonders where they all are now—when an empty hospital train arrived bound for the base, and, as I waited, streams of wounded were assisted into the station and put into the carriages. The contrast was striking in the extreme : on the one side, the healthy, singing lads whom England was hurrying out to the war ; on the other, the crippled, broken remnants returning home. The pathos of the whole scene was intensified by the continuous distant rumble of the guns—heard now for the first time—coming from over the hills which lay to the north. I tried to engage in conversation with the medical officer superintending the removal of the wounded ; but he turned out to be a most melancholy fellow, whose dismal outlook on the war did not tend to raise my spirits.

At length the bus arrived—an old London motor bus, now painted all over in dull greyish green—and conveyed me to the village of La Crêche. Here in some unexpected, providential way I found myself taken in hand by some most obliging officers of the Army Service Corps, who lent me a car to take me to my destination. We went to the wrong Ambulance at first—at Romarin, I think it was—but ultimately found the 1/1 South Midland Field Ambulance at Pont-de-Nieppe. I found most of the officers in the mess. They were apparently expecting me, for, after being introduced to the colonel, an officer took me at once to my billet. This was a comfortable little room over a grocer's shop and looking on to the square in front of the church. After leaving my overcoat and haversack there, and having a much needed wash, I went back to the mess for dinner.

A Nonconformist chaplain, the Rev. W——, had joined the Ambulance a day or so previously, and next morning we went out together to report our arrival to Divisional Headquarters at Nieppe.   Afterwards he accompanied me to Plugsteert village, where I was to meet the only other R.C. chaplain with the division, Father P——.   I found him established in the curé's home, and he told me how he had had to spend most of the preceding evening in the cellar owing to the enemy's shell fire.   The house did indeed show evident signs of having been hit, and the whole village, including the church, was severely damaged.   Father P—— proved an invaluable guide. I had arrived totally ignorant of army organisation ; companies, battalions, brigades were all Greek to me.

He threw light on all these, and explained that my particular charge would be the Gloucester and Worcester Brigade, comprising the 1/4 and 1/6 Gloucestershire battalions and the 1/7 and 1/8 Worcestershire battalions.   He told me where and how I should find them, and in general how I was to set about my business.   He also entrusted me with the duty of going over to La Crèche for the A.S.C. This I did regularly during our stay here, riding over every Friday in the beautiful cool of the summer evenings

My next visit to Plugsteert was memorable, as giving me, though very distantly, my first experience of shell fire.   I was walking back to the village across some fields, after visiting a company in an outlying farm, when I suddenly heard a sort of whining, whizzing sound over my head.   It was several times repeated before it dawned on me that these must be shells. My surmise was immediately confirmed by meeting a party of cheery soldiers carrying dixies to draw water from the village pump. They were complaining that if Fritz continued his little game they stood a small chance themselves of ever getting their tea. Luckily Fritz did not continue, so I hope they had their tea in as much peace as I had my walk home to Pont-de-Nieppe.

My first visit to the trenches took me through the famous Plugsteert Wood. I had called that morning at the headquarters of the 1/4 Gloucesters—a farm on the outskirts of the wood—and I went on from there with Colonel D——, who had kindly consented to take me with him. The day was boiling hot, and Plugsteert Wood malodorous with shallow graves. We soon passed beyond it and entered the system of breastworks which constituted the line. I duly looked through a periscope and gazed wonderingly over No Man's Land, and at the little mounds marking the German line beyond. I was—all as it should be —suddenly scared stiff by the ping of a sniper's bullet, which sounded almost at my ear; and finally I had a brief but good view of Messines Ridge, with its ruined church tower standing out white and glaring in the hot noonday sun. As I walked home that day, one thought persisted in occupying my mind, " I have stood in a front line trench and seen what it was like." For so long the word "trenches" had conveyed nothing but subjective impressions drawn mostly from the illustrated papers. Now at length I had come and seen them for myself.

Subsequently I paid two or three further visits on my own to Plugsteert Wood. On one occasion I went to see the cemetery—it was full of cemeteries—set apart for men of the Somersetshire Light Infantry— and on another I went farther afield, and after passing through what was known as White Hope Gate and visiting some of the Worcesters, I climbed up to the top of the Hill 63 which commanded a good view of the country lying north-east of us. On my way home I saw for the first time the huge notice board —which must, I am sure, have formed the original of one of Bairnsfather's famous sketches—erected by the Division from whom we had taken over this part of the line. As far as I remember the notice ran as follows :—

PLUGSTEERT WOOD. CAPTURED BY THE FOURTH DIVISION, OCTOBER 1914. HANDED OVER INTACT TO THE FORTY-EIGHTH DIVISION, APRIL 1915.

It was, I believe, only about this time that Territorial Divisions and Brigades were first numbered. Our Division became the 48th and my Brigade the 144th.

My arrival at Pont-de-Nieppe corresponded roughly with the first great gas attack at Ypres, and the medical staff were making frenzied efforts to combat this new form of warfare. We had a very energetic little deputy assistant director of medical services who was constantly fluttering round with new forms of gas mask. The first was a mere worsted pad— soaked in some chemical—and tied round the mouth with a string. The next effort was a complete mask which fitted right over the head and had a single oblong eye-piece of mica. The final form was similar to this, but had two eye-pieces instead of one oblong one, and also a mouth-piece and valve so that one could breathe out of the mask though still inhaling the air inside. This type held till the beginning of 1917, when we were first issued out with the small box respirator, a much more complicated affair.

Whilst at Pont-de-Nieppe I was beguiled into a furtive visit to Ypres. One or two officers had been discovered going there in motor ambulances and the practice had been forbidden; but on this occasion the ostensible object was merely to go to Mont Rouge and have a look from there at Ypres and the famous Hill 60 Two Irishmen—brothers, one a doctor and the other a chaplain—asked Padre W——, myself, and another doctor if we should like to go with them We started off, passed through Bailleul, and then went on and on, the road getting worse and worse, till, to my surprise, we suddenly crossed over a sort of moat, left a big shell-riddled railway station on our left and drew up in Ypres. We had barely stopped before the two brothers M'C—— were off like lightning. Padre W——, always prompt to seize opportunities, said he was determined to see the Cloth Hall at all costs, and was quickly away. M—— and myself were left rather foolishly gaping at the deserted street, and afraid to go far afield lest the two M'C——'s might return in our absence, drive off without us, and leave us stranded fifteen miles from home. Whilst we were hanging aimlessly around some Belgian soldiers suddenly emerged from a neighbouring cellar with several bottles of wine, and —perhaps to secure an unmolested retreat—offered us half a dozen which we stowed away in the car. We had not long to wait before the others returned, and, on our way home, we did actually get to the summit of Mont Rouge and see the view. It was certainly worth a visit. Ypres lying in its ruins clearly defined at our feet, and the ragged remnants of Hill 60 standing out prominently towards the south.

All this time I was gradually getting into my work, seeing my men, quite a number of whom, I found, came from Clevedon, including the brothers M—— in the 4th Gloucesters whom I had known as children, and whom I had last seen in the summer of 1912. I also looked up all the artillery I could find in the neighbourhood, and had one morning the surprising experience of seeing a howitzer fired for my special amusement. For Mass I used chiefly the fine church at Pont-de-Nieppe, and a charming little convent chapel at Plugsteert. The curé of the village was a fine type of old Belgian priest full of kindness and hospitality. His ways, however, were in some things different to ours, for I remember one Sunday morning when I was having breakfast in his house after saying Mass in the village he asked me if I should like an egg I said I should, and he simply got up and went to a cupboard, took out an egg from among several lying there and handed it to me. I was obviously expected to eat it raw, and showed myself, I am afraid, singularly inefficient at the task.

Every day a lively scene was enacted in the square beneath my window. It was a "refilling point," and morning by morning it would be crowded with lorries, wagons, and food and fodder of every description, all seemingly jumbled together in inextricable confusion. Order, however, evidently reigned, for in due course everything would gradually be divided and loaded up, and the square would be left to simmer emptily in the dust and heat of those early summer days.

Often also on bright nights I used to watch our troops coming back from their tour in the line for their five or six days' rest in billets, singing as they marched to the good old tune of "Here we are, here we are, here we are again." One of the features of their rest was a bath and clean change of underclothes. The baths—so much a wonder in those days that they were deemed worthy of a visit from Mr Balfour when he was in the neighbourhood—were in a disused brewery. Six or seven enormous vats, about 10 feet deep and the same in diameter, were filled with about 4 feet of hot water, and a dozen men or so occupied them at a time. From twelve to two, I think, they were reserved for officers, and one could have an entire vat to oneself. Our quartermaster one day, a small dapper little man, availing himself of the baths, got in with little difficulty, but, when his ablutions were completed, found himself quite unable to get out. He was imprisoned in his vast tub till his shouts attracted the attention of the old French attendant who came to his rescue.

Towards the end of our stay here, a brigade of the 9th Division—the vanguard of Kitchener's New Army—marched down into Armentières. They were as fine a body of men as one could wish to see, swinging down the long straight road, with their kilts swaying to the step, and their pipes playing.

The death in our hospital of a wounded Catholic

D

soldier; the subsequent burial out in a cemetery by a lonely farm; a few walks into Armentières, chiefly to replenish my kit till the arrival of my valise, which happily turned up before we left; several walks or rides in the hot broiling sun to the scattered farms where my men lay, to hear Confessions or bring them Holy Communion; one more visit to the trenches, this time to the 6th Gloucesters, who showed me, I remember, a new trench they had just completed, "Bristol Trench"—these form the chief remaining impressions of these early days which still survive with me.

One day at lunch Dr B—— turned to me and said, "Do you know we're moving." Moving—the possibility had never occurred to me before—"Yes, moving in two days' time." The next day I paid a final visit to Plugsteert, and on my way home had quite an exciting time, as I was turned back along the road by heavy shelling, and had to make my way over fields and ditches, leading a most unwilling horse—my horsemanship not being up to the situation—and in a fever all the time lest the shelling might switch over towards me.

I got back all right, and the following day, Thursday, 24th June, we marched off in the evening to Bailleul, and billeted for the night at a farmhouse about two miles south-west of the town. The farm had two small rooms available for sleeping in which were occupied by the colonel and senior major. The rest of us passed an excellent night in a hay-loft, with plenty of clean, sweet-smelling hay to lie on. We stayed here only one night, and marched the following evening to Vieux Berquin. This summer marching

was wholly enjoyable and like a prolonged picnic.
The days were intensely hot. One lolled lazily about,
and everywhere khaki figures lay dotted round, lying
prone on their faces in the dry grass, till the cool
evening came and we started off once more.

On our second night of trekking my wholly novel
surroundings, or possibly my supper the evening
before, brought on me a most realistic nightmare.
We were sleeping as usual in a straw-laden loft, when
—the details are still most vivid even after this long
lapse of time—I seemed to myself to be lying on the
ground with a great host of horsemen galloping
furiously right on to me ; and I remember waking up
—and waking the others up too—with a great cry
and holding out my arm as though to shield myself,
and then seeing myself lying in a great litter of hay
and straw, it was some moments before I could collect
my senses and realise where I was.

On the evening of Saturday, 26th June, about half-
past eight, we started off on a really long march
through Vieux Berquin and Merville to the outskirts
of Béthune, arriving ultimately about four in the
morning at the little village of Gonnehem. I walked
nearly all the way—except for a few miles when
one of the officers lent me his horse—and I was
thoroughly tired out by the time we reached our
billets. After some breakfast I slept till about ten,
and then got up and heard Mass in the village
church. That same evening we marched to our final
destination at Allouagne.

Here we stayed from the 27th of June till the 15th
of July. It was a picturesque country, and I had
several very pretty rides—one particularly, which I

often took through a wood to Marles-les-Mines—
visiting my battalions round about. Once or twice
I went into the then flourishing town of Béthune,
and on one occasion we all went to see Lord
Kitchener who, with the Prince of Wales, reviewed
our Division lined up on the main Lillers-Béthune
road. He looked very different to what he appeared
in pictures. He had aged considerably, and looked
heavy and sleepy as he lay back in his car.

At the beginning of July the Division had, I
believe, orders to move into the line in front of
Béthune, and one battalion got as far as Nœux-
les-Mines, where I managed to go myself in a car
with the colonel. The whole thing, however, was
cancelled, and instead, in a few days, we moved into
a neighbouring area and the Ambulance went to
Ames. On the day of the move the colonel took
Padre W—— and myself to Boulogne with him.
He was going on leave. It was a pretty run via St
Omer, and the fact that we took a wrong road only
meant that we saw more of the country parts and
the rolling hills.

We found Ames a delightful village—at any rate
for this time of the year—sunk in a hollow away from
all the main roads. I discovered from the Stations
of the Cross which he had presented to the little
village church where I used to say Mass, that Ames
was the birthplace of one of the Priors of St Hugh's
Charterhouse at Parkminster in Sussex.

We left Ames on Tuesday evening, 20th July,
marched to Lillers, and, after dining at a café there,
entrained about half-past eight. After a long
journey we ultimately got out at Mondicourt, on the

Doullens-Arras line, at half-past two in the morning, and marched from there to Sarton—a tedious march after the night in the train, and one long remembered on account of the choking dust which arose as I walked along with M—— at the tail of the column.

Sarton was an inexpressibly dull place, far removed from the rest of the Division, stuffy, dirty, and infested beyond measure with flies. Some of the officers lived in tents. My own billet tallied with the rest of the village in general unpleasantness. One cool evening I ventured to play chess with Dr W——, who apparently was a county champion at the game. We were playing in an orchard where his tent was, and after two or three moves Dr W——, who was never given to mincing words, leant back in his chair and exclaimed solemnly, " I see you have not the least notion of the very elements of the game." He then proceeded to checkmate me in a few minutes.

One afternoon Padre W—— and myself made a determined effort to get up to the line, but we got no farther than the village of Coigneux, where we met the 3rd South Midland Field Ambulance, encamped in such a delightful wood that we had to stop and have tea there. On the way back the Divisional General overtook us in his car, and gave us a welcome lift home over the hot and dusty roads.

On another occasion I bicycled painfully right up to Hebuterne itself, and was astonished to find how close I had come to the front line. On my way back, at the top of the ridge separating the villages of Hebuterne and Sailly, I got off my bicycle to watch the German shells dropping harmlessly near a French battery in action in the hollow on my left. Provided one is at a moderately safe distance, there is an extraordinary fascination in watching bursting shells, and seeing great masses of earth and columns of smoke shooting up into the air.

Eventually after Padre W—— and myself had made ineffective efforts to attach ourselves to a unit nearer the line, and so nearer our men as well, we heard with great delight that the Ambulance was going to set up an Advanced Dressing Station at the forward village of Colincamps.

CHAPTER II

NEW SCENES

On Tuesday, 3rd August, C Section of the Ambulance, commanded by Major B——, Lieut. M——, Padre W——, and myself established ourselves in the village of Colincamps. Padre W—— and I slept in the schoolhouse or Mairie—I never quite knew which it was—adjoining the church; the other two slept in a farm where the men were billeted and where we set up the A.D.S.

When the Division first took up this front by Hebuterne and Colincamps, it had relieved a Division of French troops, and for our first few days we had the pleasure of having a French artillery officer with us. He was a charming little man and a great addition to our mess. His guns were, however, withdrawn shortly after we arrived and he went with them.

We spent about three weeks at Colincamps, and, in spite of occasional shelling in the evening, we had on the whole quite a pleasant time. Only once did any shells drop immediately around our farm, and that day I happened to be out. On one occasion, however, a battery just in front of us came in for a considerable "hate." It had apparently just come

34

out from England, and the way in which it set about its business earned for it the nickname of "Fred Karno's" battery, after some famous Birmingham comedian. It certainly bought its own trouble, for, though not dug in in any way, it continued firing with an enemy aeroplane just above it, and the position was obviously spotted at once. One of the casualties from the shelling—they were happily few and I think none were killed—was a case of shell shock, the first I had seen.

It was a gunner boy, who looked not more than eighteen, absolutely overcome, quite unable to move unsupported, and sobbing like a child. I can see him still with his rosy, healthy face, sitting crying in a chair with his hands up to his eyes. One of the shells on this particular occasion killed two ducks and a goose. The gunners, as being directly responsible for the whole affair, claimed the ducks as their own and went off with them. They condescended, however, to leave us the goose, whose permanent domicile had undoubtedly been in our own yard.

Another incident of our stay at Colincamps was the first arrival on this front of one of our 12-inch guns. It established itself in an orchard just behind the church, and each time it prepared to fire it drew a swarm of soldiers around it like a football crowd.

Our first week at Colincamps was marked by continuous and heavy rains, and the trenches became so absolutely water-logged that the men used to walk about in them with nothing on but a shirt and boots. Happily the prevailing warmth of the weather made the conditions less trying than they might otherwise have been. When the weather mended I paid a visit to the trenches—about a mile and a half away over open ground—and saw my first deep German dug-out, for here we were in a little spur of the line which had been captured by the French in the preceding June.

During our stay at Colincamps I naturally used the village church for Mass. This was a comparatively new and quite pretty little building, not much damaged by shell-fire, and dedicated to St Thomas Aquinas, of whom there was a fine oil-painting above the high altar. The church will always linger in my memory as being the scene of the first Communion of a lad in the 4th Gloucesters, whom I had received into the Church at Pont-de-Nieppe. Nestling under its walls also was the lonely grave of a Warwickshire soldier whom we buried there. Besides Colincamps I used also to say Mass on Sundays at the church in Courcelles, which lay about a mile behind Towards the end of August there was a shuffling of divisional fronts, and, to our great regret, we had to hand over the A.D.S. at Colincamps to the 4th Division. It was taken over by the 11th Field Ambulance.

Our party returned to Arqueves — where the Ambulance had moved since we had been at Colincamps—and I remained there a week. Arqueves was even more out of the world than Sarton had been, and I was delighted at the opportunity of leaving it, when a new A.D.S. was opened at Foncquevillers. This was opened on Thursday, 2nd September, in the first house on the left as one enters the village from Souastre. The same party formed it as had

1·

been at Colincamps, except that we had fewer men with us, and Padre W—— was away on leave. Major B—— and the colonel went up together in the afternoon to arrange matters with the French unit from whom we were taking over, and I arrived later, going in the Ford car—which I had prevailed on the senior major to lend me—via Authie, Pas, and Souastre. I got out at Souastre—which I found full of French soldiers—and lifting my bicycle out of the car, biked the rest of the way into Foncquevillers. I met the colonel returning home, and I have no doubt that, seeing me on a bicycle, he was under the impression I had dutifully bicycled the whole way from Arqueves, and I was thankful I had got out of the Ford when I had and sent it home.

Arriving at Foncquevillers I found the French Medical Officers had received us with open arms. Major B—— and I were invited to dinner, and they provided an excellent meal, turned out in that inimitable French style which seems to produce a six-course dinner out of a tiny oil stove. After dinner the major joined them in a game of bridge, and I sat in a comfortable chair and looked at copies of the illustrated papers. Later we said good-night and good-bye as they were to leave in the early hours of the morning.

Lieut. M—— and his party were due to arrive about 1.30 in the morning, and the major and I walked out along the Souastre road to meet them. As we got to know the enemy's temper better, groups of men would be up and down that road continuously day and night, smoking and laughing; but to-night as we emerged from the village we were peremptorily told by the sentry to put out our cigarettes as they were likely to draw shell-fire. At length we heard the tramp of feet in the darkness, and were soon leading back our party to our new home.

For nearly six months Foncquevillers was indeed to be my home, and I shall always have the pleasantest memories of the time I spent there, and of this the most comfortable winter of the war. September and October were lovely months, mild and warm—as they so often are in France—so that during our first weeks we used to sit out in the overgrown tangled garden which lay behind the house ; and I remember, one September evening, hearing the officers reading out to the men—paraded in a neighbouring orchard—a despatch from Lord French, announcing that we were " on the eve of great operations." It was the eve of the famous Loos and Champagne offensives which, like those of Ypres in the autumn of 1917, cost so many thousand lives and achieved comparatively little. As the evenings began to get cold and dark we abandoned the garden for the mess-room, always warm and cosy and bright, for happily the days of shortage in fuel and oil were not yet.

Life at Foncquevillers was, for me, regular in the extreme. I was now working with the Warwick or 143rd Brigade, consisting of the 1/5, 1/6, 1/7, and 1/8 Battalions of the Royal Warwickshire Regiment. Of these, two battalions would occupy the trenches ; one battalion would have two companies in Foncquevillers and two at the Château de la Haie about a mile behind ; and one battalion would be in rest billets at Bavencourt, a village about a mile behind

the Château. As there was a general move round
every eight days, I managed to see all the battalions
in turn. Every Sunday I said a nine o'clock Mass
at Bayencourt, and one at half-past ten at Foncquevillers, every Saturday evening I heard Confessions
from six to seven at Bayencourt, and from half-past
seven to eight at Foncquevillers; and once every
week I used to say a Mass at the Château de la
Haie. The day varied every week, for I always
arranged to be there the morning of the day before
the men went back into the line.

The chapel at Foncquevillers was my constant
delight. It had been handed over to me by the
French, and consisted simply of a barn with one end
raised slightly, and with a finely carved wooden altar
rescued from the ruins of the village church. In a
convenient nook about half-way down, where the
barn opened out to a width of about twenty feet, was
a little screened-off recess, with a chest of drawers
and a prie-dieu, which acted admirably as a sacristy
and confessional. My first care was to get a lock for
the tabernacle. This the Engineers did for me at
once. I then brought a little oil lamp from Pas, and
everything was ready for the Blessed Sacrament which
remained in the village till I left. In spite of its
destitute bareness and simplicity my little chapel
was admired by all. If the tiles got broken—as they
frequently did at nights by machine-gun bullets—
men were promptly available with ladders to replace
them. A major in the artillery gave me pictures to
decorate the walls, and a man out of the Warwicks,
back from leave, presented me with a fine altar cover
which he had got from a Convent at home as a gift

for the chapel. Often on a dark winter's night I would go in there and discern by the dim light of the tiny lamp the figure of one or other of my Catholic boys kneeling in prayer ; and on Sunday mornings it would fill up quite considerably, my own congregation being swelled by several men from the 37th Division who were holding the line on our immediate left. As a chapel it was not, however, destined to outlast the war, for when I saw it later it was absolutely in ruins, though the altar was still there.

Just as my weekly round was fixed, so was my daily round also. After Mass, breakfast, and a smoke I used to wander round the village, and was almost certain to meet someone or other I was anxious to see. Failing that I would make my way to the men's billets. In the afternoons I usually went over either to the Château de la Haie or Bayencourt to see the men there, both artillery and infantry, and sometimes I would pay a visit to Rossignol Farm,'a big building standing out on a prominent spur of the hill above Coigneux, and which was the home of some Engineers. Occasionally, of course, one went farther afield ; and in fact, in the early days of our stay at Foncque-villers, one of the doctors and myself got once or twice as far as Doullens. We had then two motor ambulances at our disposal ; but such luxury did not last long, and we were reduced to one, which of course had to stand by all day in case of casualties, and so was not available. Shortly after Christmas, also, I had occasion to ride over once or twice to the village of St Amand, lying a mile or so north of Souastre, to see some heavy gunners there. It used to be a most pleasant ride, for there was a soft track of nearly two miles running parallel to the Souastre-Foncquevillers road, and nothing could be more delightful than to gallop home along it in the glow of a bright winter's afternoon, with the prospect of a warm room and tea awaiting one at the other end.

Whilst the evenings were still light I used to ride or even bicycle over to Bayencourt on Saturdays, using the track which went direct from the Château de la Haie. With winter rains and frost, however, this track became absolutely impassable to anything but foot traffic, and many were the dark rainy nights on which I used to make my way over the duck-board track recently laid down to the little dimiy lit church at Bayencourt. If the weather was fine I used often to cycle as far as the Château where the road ended abruptly, and, leaving my bike there, pursue my way on foot, picking up my bicycle on the way home. On approaching Foncquevillers I used often to be hurried on my way by the zip-zip of machine-gun bullets. Almost every evening there used to be a regular tornado of bullets whistling over our heads, and I remember being caught one night at the entrance to the village by such a continuous roar of fire as I had never heard before, and which drove me to cower for shelter under the lee-wall of a little shrine which stood near. There was really, however, little danger as for months the angle of fire was too high, and almost all the bullets, doubtless destined for the village streets, would either pass right over and land into the empty fields behind, or lose themselves among the roofs. Only towards the end did the enemy's machine-gun fire become in any way effective, and even then casualties were never high.

After we had been in the line for about six weeks the enemy began to harass us with "minen-werfers," popularly known as "minnies." The first night they came over, the doctor doing duty at the A.D.S. at the time—the doctors and men worked in monthly reliefs from the main ambulance at Arqueves—had taken the opportunity of a car going to Amiens and back to take a day off. There were always one or two other medical officers in the village, in case of an emergency, and he was not expected back till after dinner. We had just finished this meal and were talking to some officers at the door of the house when we heard a terrific explosion from the direction of the line. It was followed by several others in quick succession, then silence. We had heard nothing so violent before, and the officers went back to their billets to find out what had happened. We at the Dressing Station were soon to know, for in a few minutes the Adjutant of the 7th Warwicks came hurrying in to prepare us for the arrival of several casualties. Happily, the doctor had just got back and he was soon busily at work. The casualties, however, turned out to be less than had been thought. Three were killed, and they laid them temporarily in the mortuary outside my own little room which adjoined the dressing-room. The latter was a busy scene till late that night, when eventually all the wounded were dressed and evacuated. Though from this time onwards we were constantly troubled by "minnies" the loss of life they inflicted was really slight. On this occasion, out of twelve rounds fired, only one, the last, caused any casualties at all. It dropped short of our lines and fell on to an occupied sap-head out in "No Man's" Land. Subsequently I remember a sergeant being brought in, with one of his legs almost entirely severed near the hip by a piece of "minnie." He died whilst his wounds were being dressed. Apart, however, from isolated cases like these, it was more the terrific explosion they made than the harm they did which caused minnies to be held in such dread.

Much of the enemy activity was undoubtedly due to our own offensive tactics. Originally when the French held it, this had been a particularly quiet spot. But now we stirred up strife by making raids. The 6th Gloucesters carried out a most successful raid just below us at Hebuterne, and subsequently the Warwicks revenged a quiet little operation of the enemy, which had resulted in the loss of one of our new Lewis guns, by making a big raid of their own, in front of Foncquevillers.

During these months my visits to the trenches became much more frequent From our door to the front line was barely a ten minutes' walk, and I used to find in this as in all fairly quiet sectors, that the trenches were by far the best place for seeing the men, and that they appreciated a visit there far more than one in back areas.

On Thursday, 10th February 1916, we left Foncquevillers. Our place was taken by another Ambulance of the Division, and we took over from them the A.D.S. at Hebuterne. Here the 145th Brigade was in the line, comprising the 1/5

Gloucesters, 1/4 Oxford and Bucks, 1st Bucks, and the 1/5 Royal Berks. Hitherto the 144th and 145th Brigades had held the line here alternately, but now the 144th Brigade was moved up to the left of the Warwick Brigade.

At Hebuterne we were not nearly so comfortable as at Foncquevillers. I slept in a very bare, cold room next to our mess, but only accessible from it by going out into the garden behind or the road in front and turning into the next yard. Almost every night I was disturbed by our own guns, which invariably started firing about eleven o'clock and went on for nearly an hour. There would generally be some retaliation on the part of the enemy, which used to keep me in two minds as to whether or no I should get up and take refuge in a cellar near by, where the M.O. of some gunners used to sleep.

Father P—— was now in charge of Bayencourt and Foncquevillers, and I took his place in serving the church at Sailly au Bois.

I also said Mass every Sunday, for the troops in Hebuterne, in a wonderful deep cellar some thirty feet down, and capable of holding nearly a hundred. The Engineers fitted it with two little arc lamps, and besides being used for services, it came in most useful for one or two concerts we had there as well.

Life at Hebuterne was on the whole similar to that at Foncquevillers. Every Saturday evening I used to be at Sailly Church for Confessions, and on Sunday mornings, after a nine o'clock Mass at Hebuterne, I used to ride over to Sailly for Mass at half-past ten. The early part of the winter of 1916

F

was very severe, and I shall always associate
Hebuterne with several walks in biting cold and
sleet along the bare bleak road which led over
the crest of the hill behind the village and dipped
down into Sailly. Sometimes I would go over to
Courcelles to see the artillery billeted around there.
The curé at Courcelles was one I had known well
since our stay at Colincamps.

There are many varied types of the village curé
in France, but he at Courcelles was one for whom
I had an admiration and esteem amounting to real
affection. Living in extreme poverty, his hospitality
was nevertheless full of dignity and charm. I went
over to see him again on the eve of the 1st of July
and found his house and church deserted. Stress
of war had finally compelled him, like all the other
inhabitants, to seek shelter elsewhere.

Another change in the divisional fronts led to the
A.D.S. at Colincamps being reopened by us, and
Lieut. M—— of the Ambulance was sent to take
charge. Though I still continued to live at Hebuterne,
I used to go over to Colincamps from time to time to
see him as he was the only officer there. On one
occasion I accompanied him up to a bearer-party
post at La Sucrerie, about a mile nearer the line, to
meet two or three casualties who were expected
down. We saw two men, but we were expecting a
wounded officer also, and we went up to the entrance
of the cellar, where the post lived, to see if there was
any sign of him. We met an officer there and asked
him if he had seen a wounded officer being brought
down. "Oh," he said, "I'm the officer." On asking
him where he had been hit, he pointed to his heart

and said " here." Undoing his shirt, there we saw the wound clearly enough, just above his heart, and the bullet still plainly visible bulging out under the skin. Though obviously a spent bullet, his escape had been a narrow one, but, apart from a little faintness, he did not seem much the worse, and walked back with us to Colincamps.

The 144th Brigade had returned from the north of Foncquevillers to this part of the line, and whilst here they were considerably troubled by the use of poison gas, which the enemy was now putting over on this front for the first time. The first serious gas case I saw was at our main ambulance, now moved to Bus. The man was breathing heavily, and his face was a livid purple colour The sight of him lying out there between life and death, with thousands of spring crocuses breaking out into life around him in the bright morning sun, forms one of my most vivid recollections in all the war.

From Hebuterne I took my first " leave" to England, leaving on 27th March and returning on 8th April. The acquaintance I had always aimed at making with the artillery served me in good stead on my return journey. I had arrived at Authie on the night of 7th April, and stayed there till the following morning, when I started out to walk the six miles or so to Hebuterne. I had got as far as the village of St Leger, when I met a sergeant-major whom I had last seen up in the line with the guns. He was staying now at the horse lines, and immediately offered me a horse and orderly to take me up to my destination, an offer I gladly accepted.

Shortly after my return from " leave" I came

across my brother F—— who was chaplain to the 1st
Inniskillings in the 29th Division, which had just
come to France from Gallipoli.   We met quite
accidentally in the streets of Mailly-Maillet and had
lunch together there, and subsequently he rode over
to see me at Hebuterne.

As at Foncquevillers so now I used to pay frequent
visits to the trenches.   I was going round one
morning with the M.O. of the 6th Gloucesters—we
had again handed over the line in front of Colincamps to another division, and the 144th Brigade
was back at Hebuterne, alternating with the 145th—
when we came across a group of young officers
looking over the parapet with glasses, and studying
the lie of the land with a view to a raid.   We had
barely left them a minute before several shells came
over in quick succession all round us, and almost
immediately we heard the cry—which was to become
afterwards so painfully familiar to me—for stretcher-
bearers.   The doctor and his orderly hastened back
and found young P. N——, whose two elder brothers
I got to know so well later, had been badly
wounded.   I made my way back to Battalion Headquarters, and whilst there heard that N—— had died
almost immediately.   He was buried in the little
cemetery that lay behind the village.

With the warm weather Hebuterne became far
more pleasant.   We used to sit out in front of our
house in the afternoon sun, and this period always
recalls to my mind a French book of Alphonse
Daudet's I read and much appreciated at the time,
Robert Helmont, with its wonderfully vivid pictures
of certain lesser incidents of the 1870 War

During all this period we were engaged, though as yet unwittingly, in preparing for the great attack of July 1st. At Foncquevillers, Hebuterne, and, as we afterwards found, at Colincamps, the building of shell-proof Dressing Stations was being vigorously pushed forward. At Hebuterne the spot selected was just outside the village on the Sailly road. It was not really a very sound place to choose as it was almost on a cross-roads and, even as early as this, subjected to more shell-fire than other equally convenient sites. In fact, when I visited Hebuterne later, I found that the elaborately built shelters on the Sailly road had been given up, and the Dressing Station established further up the village street, in a reinforced cellar, close to my own original billet.

My last fortnight at Hebuterne was, I think, the pleasantest period of all. Lieut. M—— and myself were there alone with about twenty men. Pending the completion of the new Dressing Station, we spent a lot of time reinforcing our own one with sand-bags—as at no time had it been really safe—and in generally improving it, and I used to lend a willing if unskilful hand in dressing the wounded. By day casualties were very few, and when a wounded man did arrive he used to receive as much concentrated attention as, in times of heavy fighting, he would hardly have received till reaching the base; and on one occasion, with the aid of another doctor, we went so far as to do an amputation Among the sad cases we had in the dressing station was that of a gunner who had come up from the wagon lines for the day to see the guns in action, and was wounded by the premature explosion of one of our own shells. He died a short time afterwards before he reached the hospital

On Tuesday, the 1st of May, we left Hebuterne and rejoined the main body of the Ambulance at Souastre, where it had moved a few weeks previously from Bus.

CHAPTER III

PEACE BEFORE THE STORM

AT 4 A.M. on the morning of Thursday, 3rd May, we left Souastre and, following on behind the 144th Brigade, marched via Couin, Authie, Marieux, and Beauquesne to Beauval, which we reached about half-past ten. Our billets here were excellent, and as the whole brigade was in the town, I had quite a large congregation for Mass on Sunday in the fine church here. However, as there was already an R.C. chaplain attached to the Casualty Clearing Station in the town, I took the opportunity of accompanying Lieut. M—— to the little village of Gezaincourt, a few miles away, where a section of our Ambulance was to take charge of the divisional baths. The 143rd or Warwick Brigade took up its quarters in the village a few days later, and as Father P—— was not there at the time, it was an advantage for me to be on the spot.

M—— and I lived in a tent, pitched just inside the grounds of the local château, by the side of a mill stream. Immediately in front of our tent the ground fell steeply away to the water, and, a few yards higher up, the stream could be crossed by a narrow plank bridge, supporting the weir gates, which

led over the mill-wheel into the mill-house itself on
the opposite bank   Here our two batmen lived.
The people of the mill were extremely kind to us,
and allowed us to use their kitchen stove for cooking
on. Our meals were brought over from the house, and
I used to watch with some anxiety M——'s servant,
with a plate of soup in each hand, balancing himself
across the plank over the weir, crawling through a
barbed wire fence, and then ascending the very
slippery bank up to our tent. A blast on my whistle
was the signal for the next course, and this was the
only occasion throughout the war I ever had of using it.
In spite of lots of rain we spent here a most enjoyable
ten days. We kept our horses in Gezaincourt and had
several very pleasant rides together. On Sundays,
besides Mass in the village church—where I met
once more those Warwickshire lads I had got to know
and love so well at Foncquevillers—I used also to
ride over to the neighbouring village of Hem to say
Mass there for the Engineers.

One night we were both invited out to dinner by
P——, who had spent a few days with us once at
Hebuterne. He was now M.O. to an Entrenching
Battalion living up at Longuevillette, a good half-
hour's walk away. It was rather a strange dinner
party—I hardly know why—and afterwards they all
settled down to play bridge, leaving M—— and myself to look on   This we did for some time, with
several protestations of interest, till I could endure
it no longer, and we excused ourselves, said good-
night, and walked home in the moonlight.   '

About this time a big change took place as far as
I personally was concerned, for I was transferred

from the Ambulance and attached to the 1/6
Gloucesters to act as R.C. chaplain to the 144th
Brigade. Father P—— had the Warwick Brigade,
and Father G——, who had joined us the preceding
August, went to the 145th Brigade. Accordingly
one bright May morning I said good-bye to M——
and our peaceful life at Gezaincourt, and rode off
towards the line. On reaching Couin I went to the
transport lines of the Gloucesters, and got a fresh
horse there and an orderly who came up with me
to Hebuterne, where the battalion was in the
trenches.

I arrived about tea-time and found Battalion Headquarters in a house at the southern extremity of the
village The Battalion was commanded at the time
by Lieut.-Col. M——, and I shall never forget his
saying towards the end of tea, " Well, I don't know
where we are going to put you. I expect you'd better
have one of the pig-styes." It sounded far from
pleasant, but I soon discovered the " pig-styes " to
be quite an aristocratic quarter. Needless to say,
all trace of their original tenants had gone, and now
they consisted of two little chambers with reinforced
roofs and sand-bagged entrance, fitted with beds and
chairs, and extremely cool and clean. One was
already occupied by a major, the other was handed
over to me, and I was soon comfortably installed
there.

I joined the Gloucesters at Hebuterne on Friday,
19th May. We left the village on the following
Wednesday. My impressions of these first days with
the Battalion are of beautiful warm sunny weather, a
far better mess than I had so far been accustomed

to, two rounds of the trenches, once by night with Major M'F——, the second-in-command, once in the early hours of the morning with the adjutant, and finally, a constantly running but excellent gramophone.

We left Hebuterne on the 24th of May, and went to a bivouac camp behind Sailly, and between that village and Coigneux. We spent ten days here. For Mass on Sunday I used a fairly large hut lent me by one of the Field Ambulances whose camp adjoined ours. My own home consisted of an army bivouac, which I folded down at one end, leaving a length of about eight feet. It was about four feet wide, and along the centre about three feet high. I used to crawl inside and make myself quite comfortable. Our mess was in a hut. The fear of night bombing was as yet unknown, and the consequent need also of screening lights, so that from the top of the hill overlooking the camp it was quite a pretty sight, of an evening, to watch the countless little lights glimmering out into the darkness from each bivouac or hut not only of our own Battalion but also of the other three who lay alongside ours. One day, whilst we were here, there was a torrential downpour of rain, accompanied by high wind and thunder. The Observation balloon behind Coigneux broke loose and floated over our camp, vaguely visible in the clouds, and whilst we were watching that, an aeroplane in distress came surging into the valley and landed just above us. The occupants of the latter were unhurt, and the balloon—minus, of course, its observers who had come down in their parachutes—came ultimately to earth just in our own lines behind Hebuterne.

On 1st June we moved to billets—and very good ones, too, I remember—at Authie ; and the afternoon we arrived I played the only game of tennis I got during the war, on a red gravel court behind the Château, which was occupied at the time by a Field Ambulance.

Next day we moved to Gezaincourt.   The Corps Commander overtook us on the march, riding down on us with his escort, in a high state of dudgeon, declaring the Battalion was " bulging badly," in other words, not keeping its exact alignment on the road. He singled out Major M'F——, who was riding beside me at the rear of the Battalion, wanted to know what he was doing there, and hurried him up to the head of the column.   After finding fault generally, he turned round to Major M'F—— and remarked quite pleasantly before riding away, " You know, a Corps Commander must find something to do."

We stayed two nights at Gezaincourt, camped out in a field, and on Sunday, 4th June, marched to Oneux, about seven miles north-west of Abbeville. The whole brigade spent most of its time in vigorous training   Of the other battalions one was quite close to us at Neuville, one at Coulonvillers, and one at Maison Roland, and I used to ride round and visit them, and, as far as possible, arrange Mass and Confessions for them in their respective villages.   One day I visited the Abbey Church of St Riquier, a magnificent old building, once sacked by the English during the Hundred Years' War, as the curé at Oneux laughingly reminded me.   Two or three times, also, I went into Abbeville, and on one occasion I visited the battlefield of Crecy which lay a few miles to the north of us. The only monument I could find commemorating the battle was a tiny and comparatively modern one, set up on the little wayside road which led from the main one into the Crecy woods.

On Monday the 12th we moved to Yvrench, and two days later to Outrebois, near Doullens. On this occasion—the move was a very sudden one—I rode on early with the billeting officer to fix up the new billets. It was a desperate rush, hurrying from one house to another—it was before the time of Town Majors and numbered billets—and I remember—it seems now like a sort of a dream—attempting to fix Battalion Headquarters in a neighbouring Château surrounded by dense woods, and the vision suddenly appearing of the beautiful young châtelaine accompanied by her two children. Though the accommodation was forthcoming we decided ultimately it was too far away, and that we had better leave Headquarters where we had originally fixed it. Then, as we returned to the village, we met the staff captain of our brigade who told us the Battalion would not, after all, be in till two or three hours later than we had expected. It did arrive at length, and we had dinner about midnight. Afterwards it hardly seemed worth while going to bed as on this, of all nights, "Summer Time" came in, and we had to put our watches on an hour and then start at four o'clock on our next march. This time we returned once more to familiar ground, and encamped just behind Coigneux at the foot of Couin Hill.

Everywhere preparations for the great July offen-

sive were in full swing. Long lines of guns and
ammunition wagons, including French ones, would
pass our camp at the trot every evening on the way
to their forward positions, and everywhere along the
roads ammunition dumps were springing up and
light railways being constructed.

We stopped at Coigneux a week, and then on
Thursday, 22nd June, we returned to our old bivouacs
in the valley behind Sailly. The weather was heavy
with rain and the trenches bad, and we used to see on
relief days groups of unfortunate men staggering from
the line covered from head to foot in mud. We remained here during the bombardment which preceded
the great attack. Our own valley was curiously still,
the waves of sound seemed to pass over us, and it
escaped also all hostile shelling, though Sailly village
and the roads leading up to it were shelled constantly,
and the village church was no longer safe to use.

On the morning of the attack, Saturday, 1st July,
we marched away to Mailly-Maillet, hearing as we
went constant rumours of success; how Gommecourt
Wood was surrounded, and Serre in our hands. Our
subsequent movements are best explained by briefly
referring to the events and plans of that momentous
day. By noon it was definitely ascertained that the
attack on our whole Corps front had failed, and that
the troops were back in their old line. At the conference held that afternoon at Divisional Headquarters
it was decided that the 144th Brigade should renew the
attack on Beaumont Hamel that night. Everything
was arranged as well as the short time admitted, and
then, a few minutes only before zero hour, the attack
was cancelled

When the colonel came back to the camp after the conference, we received orders to prepare to go up the line at dusk. I then joined myself temporarily to the 2nd South Midland Field Ambulance and went up with them to the A.D.S. which we opened at Vitermont near Englebelmer. Here I intended remaining during the battle. I was just resting preparatory to the opening of the attack when the news reached us that it was cancelled. Next morning I returned to Mailly-Maillett and rejoined the Gloucesters who had come back there also. That same afternoon we marched back to our bivouacs at Sailly. My own brigade was intact, but the Division had lent two Battalions of the Warwicks to the, I think, 4th Division. These were engaged in the attack on 1st July, and, though fighting excellently, suffered, alas, tremendous casualties, and many good friends of mine never came back.

We remained behind Sailly for two nights, and then the Battalion went into the already familiar line in front of Colincamps. After spending one night with the 1/2 South Midland Field Ambulance at Sailly, I went up next morning to the A.D.S. at Colincamps and remained there whilst the Battalion was in the trenches. The A.D.S. was no longer now in a farmhouse, but in strongly built dug-outs on the road out of the village to Sailly.

I went up to the trenches two or three times whilst the Battalion was there. From an observation post near headquarters one could clearly see lines of British dead lying out on the rising ground towards Serre, and every day dead were being brought out of the trenches themselves and deposited in the already overcrowded cemeteries, where, in strange stark attitudes, they lay and awaited burial.

On Sunday, 9th July, the Battalion was relieved and I rejoined it at Courcelles, a village now destitute of inhabitants and subject to shell-fire. On Wednesday, the battalion went back again into the line, and I once more took up my abode at the A.D.S. One evening, 14th July, a man was brought in who had been lying out in front of our lines since the attack on the 1st. Wounded in the legs and unable to move, he had kept himself alive by eating his own iron rations and those of the dead around him, and drinking rain-water collected in his steel helmet. He was weak naturally and emaciated, and his wounds had become gangrenous, but his pulse was good and we were not without hope of his ultimate recovery. That same evening the Battalion was relieved and marched back to a camp just west of Couin, and that night I rejoined them.

CHAPTER IV

SUMMER AND WINTER ON THE SOMME

(1) *Summer.*

ON Saturday, 15th July, we left our camp at Couin and proceeded in buses to the great Somme battle-field. We got out near Senlis, and walking through the village reached the rising ground above it, and there we waited. Far in the distance we could see the flame and smoke of battle eddying round Ovillers, a strange sight, like some painted drop-scene at a theatre, which was soon to rise and let us into the heart of things. The colonel and Major C—— were away at a conference in the neighbouring village of Bouzincourt, and as yet it was uncertain whether or no we were to move that night, and so in suspense we waited.

Presently young Major C—— came galloping back across the open full of excitement, and announced joyously that we were to move forward at once, and that the colonel would meet us in the village. A few minutes later we were streaming over the open fields into Bouzincourt. That night I spent in the village while the battalion went on to the "Quarries" east of Aveluy. Next morning, after Mass in the

14

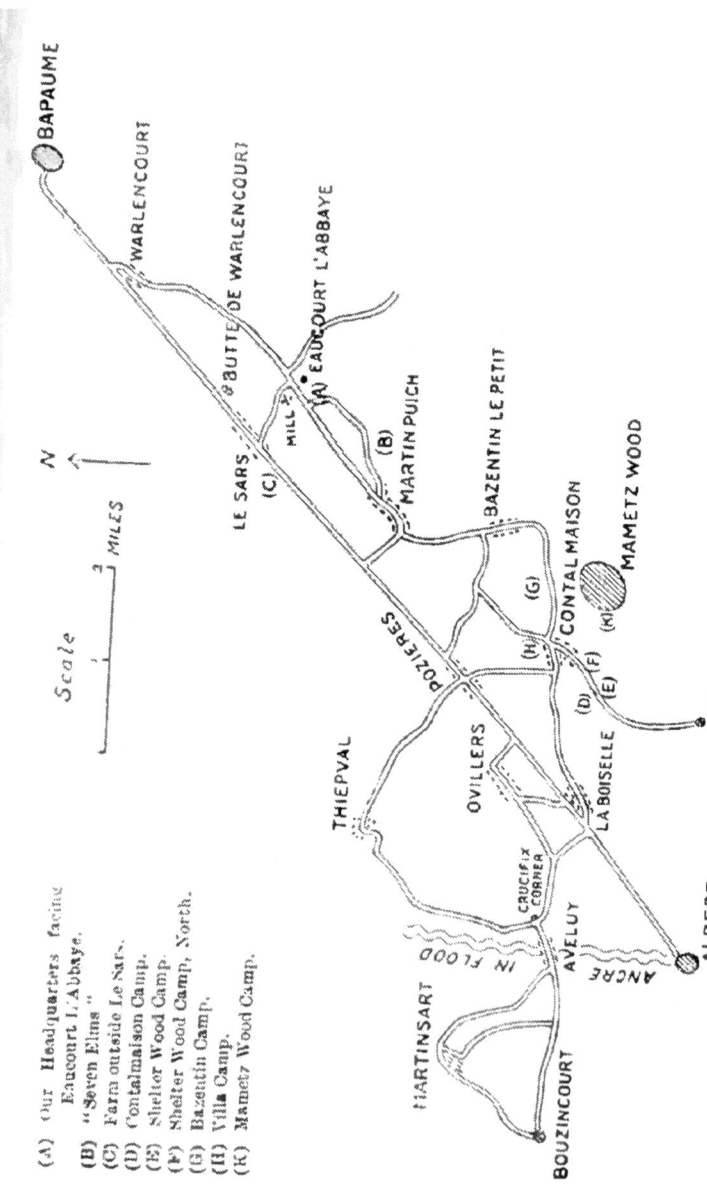

(A) Our Headquarters facing
    Eaucourt L'Abbaye.
(B) "Seven Elms"
(C) Farm outside Le Sars.
(D) Contalmaison Camp.
(E) Shelter Wood Camp.
(F) Shelter Wood Camp, North.
(G) Bazentin Camp.
(H) Villa Camp.
(K) Mametz Wood Camp.

SKETCH MAP SHOWING OUR POSITIONS ON THE SOMME, JULY TO DECEMBER 1916.

11

village church, I went up to an A.D.S. between Aveluy
and the "Quarries" at a spot known as Crucifix
Corner, and arranged to transfer myself there next
day. Accordingly on Monday I made my way
again through Martinsart Wood—bristling with heavy
guns—and Aveluy village, to the Dressing Station,
and took up my abode in an excellent dug-out quite
close to where we messed, and overlooking the flooded
stream of the Ancre where we bathed. Here I
remained till Wednesday week, and during all these
days there was constant fighting going on through
and beyond Ovillers, and the stream of casualties
was continuous.

Whilst we were here the Battalion received its first
draft of Derby recruits. Some of them had had but
the briefest of training. Their absolute ignorance
of war conditions was humorously pathetic. One
innocently asked where the cake was for tea ;
another inquired as to the nearest brine-baths,
which he had been accustomed to take for his
rheumatism. However, in spite of their initial
rawness, they soon developed into excellent fighting
soldiers.

My own Battalion made its first attack on, I think,
the 21st July. The evening opened with a terrific
bombardment, which went echoing and re-echoing
over the desolate valleys and hills. All through the
night I remained in the Dressing Station, helping as
far as I could. The place was a regular shambles,
full of wounded, with stretcher cases lying in the
open outside, and all through the night the stream of
stricken humanity flowed unceasing under the gaunt
outstretched arms of the great crucifix which marked

the cross-roads where we worked. Dawn broke at length, a beautiful summer morning, fresh and cool; but there was no respite till well on in the day, when the rush of wounded slowly subsided and the hard-worked doctors and orderlies were able to take some rest.

The casualties in my own Battalion, both in men and officers, were very heavy, nearly four hundred, I think. Among them was an officer, Lieut. S——, who had got his commission from the ranks when we were at Oneux. So far he had had no opportunity of buying himself a uniform, and some of the other officers had lent him tunic and puttees, etc. He was badly wounded in this attack, and was found by our adjutant walking back, in an almost dying condition, along the trench, having refused a stretcher as long as he could move at all. All he said was, "I'm so sorry, N——, I'm afraid I've spoilt your coat"; in a few hours he was dead.

What I think was a genuine case of shell-shock being cured by a subsequent shock occurred whilst we were here. A man in a complete state of collapse, unable either to walk or speak, was sent off by motor ambulance on a stretcher with several other wounded. As the car crossed the bridge over the Ancre, and was ascending the hill into Aveluy, a red-hot fragment of bursting shell struck the petrol tank and set it alight. In an instant the whole car, with its dry canvas sheeting, was a mass of flames. The shell-shock case was out of the car in a moment, and rendered the driver the greatest assistance in getting the other wounded safely away.

I remember how it was now, for the first time,

that I saw our men lying out dead on the battlefield. Going up once to Ovillers the man I was with said, " If you look over this bank, sir, you'll see our fellows lying out there," and, gratifying that morbid curiosity we all occasionally display, I looked over the bank and saw them. It is a sight one does not soon forget.

Whilst I was at Crucifix Corner I said Mass once or twice in the church at Aveluy. It was badly knocked about, though still serviceable in dry weather. Among my tiny congregation were some cyclists, detached from the 36th Divison, who lived by the A.D.S. and acted as escort for the prisoners of war.

On Wednesday, 26th July, the Battalion was relieved and I rejoined it at Bouzincourt. On Thursday afternoon we marched to Hedauville, on Friday to Arqueves, on Saturday to Beauval—Sir Douglas Haig coming out from his Château near Beauquesne and watching us march by—and finally on Sunday, leaving Beauval about three in the morning, we marched to Fransu, where we arrived about eleven o'clock These marches were really very pleasant. My place was always in the rear of the Battalion, where I used as a rule to ride with the Doctor and Second-in-Command. The early starts, though trying at the moment, really paid, as it usually meant getting into billets early before the full heat of the day. On our way to Fransu from Beauval we had an hour's halt for breakfast, somewhere between Fienvillers and Bernaville.

Fransu proved to be a most delightful spot, redolent in my mind of golden corn-fields, rich orchards, and beautiful woods, all lying out under brilliant uninterrupted sunshine The surrounding country and villages, Domart in particular, were wonderfully pretty.

Major M'F——, the Doctor, and I preferred life in the open to stuffy billets, and so we arranged to sleep in the orchard behind the mess. They two shared a tent and I had a bivouac to myself. The early morning was our one dangerous period, for at that time certain adventurous young calves would prowl around our home, stepping on to the tent or pushing and nosing into my bivouac. In the end we were forced to fence ourselves in.

Of the other battalions, one was at Surcamps, one was at Francqueville and one in the Bois de Ribeaucourt, and I used to ride around as usual to fix up Mass and Confessions for them. The church at Fransu, though very small, was extremely pretty. The interior was of white stone and vaulted, and, what one valued more than anything else, spotlessly clean. The curé was an amusingly pompous old gentleman, very kindly disposed, however, towards me and the Company officers who had their mess in his house.

Whilst we were at Fransu a service of motor lorries was arranged to take officers into Abbeville. One afternoon, after the bus had gone, some stores being very urgently required by the battalion—paint, I remember, and cocoa—I went into Abbeville on the brigade despatch rider's motor bike, sitting on the carrier behind We got to the outskirts of Abbeville in about half an hour, and there I got off, and going into a Flying Corps camp on the roadside, borrowed a clothes-brush and tried to regain my normal appear-

ance, for I was covered from head to foot in white
dust.   After making myself more or less respectable
I sallied forth into the town, made all the purchases
I wanted, and then hired a cab and went round to
the various shops collecting my numerous parcels.
These I safely deposited in the returning Officer's
bus, in which I travelled back.   On arriving at La
Haie Farm near Surcamps, where the bus stopped,
I was met by the driver of our mess-cart, and, with
his help, transferred all my parcels into his cart.
Then we both got in and jogged home together over
the fields.

I had occasion once to visit the family in La Haie
Farm, consisting of Madame and her two daughters.
They used to look after the village church at
Surcamps, and when I had said Mass there one
morning they invited me to their house to breakfast.
As a matter of fact I had arranged to have breakfast
with the Battalion in the village, but on my way
home I called at the farm.   Madame, it appeared,
had a daughter who was a nun in England, and they
were much interested to hear I knew the Convent
where she was staying.

On Wednesday, 9th August, we left Fransu and
marched to Candas.   We arrived hot and dusty in
the afternoon, and rejoiced to be able to indulge in a
delicious bathe in a big open-air swimming-bath
rigged up by the R.F.C.

Next day we moved to Puchevillers on the main
road running from Marieux to Amiens.   We stayed
two nights here.   One afternoon a Flying Corps
equipment officer, who had, I fancy, once been with
the Battalion in England, called to see us in his car.

Before leaving, as he was going on towards Marieux and would pass a big canteen on his way, he offered to get us any stores we might want, and we arranged to send our mess corporal with him. Someone went out to warn Corporal G—— to get ready, and a few minutes later I saw him strolling leisurely out of the yard in his shirt sleeves. When the officer finally rose to go, his car was nowhere to be found. Corporal G—— wittingly or not, I can't say, had apparently misunderstood the message, and instructed the driver to take him at once to the canteen, wait whilst he brought the stores we wanted, and then drive him back again; and there was nothing for it but to await his return.

On Saturday, the 12th, we left Puchevillers and marched to a camp just west of Bouzincourt. That night we slept out in the open in our valises, and I remember the horrid sensation of being wakened in the early morning by the sound of rain pattering down on the canvas cover. The following day the Battalion went into the line beyond Ovillers, and I stopped the night with the "details" at the Transport Lines just east of Bouzincourt. Next morning, 14th August, I took up my abode again at the A.D.S. by Crucifix Corner, which had once more been taken over by the 1/1 South Midland Field Ambulance.

At this time trench to trench attacks were being pushed on daily and almost hourly, and casualties were continually coming in On one afternoon two anti-aircraft gunner officers, four of their men, Padre W——, and myself went up the line to try and get in some wounded who were still lying out. We went up to Ovillers in a car from Crucifix Corner, got out at the entrance to the village, and left the car at a Bearer Post. Then we pushed forward on foot, through endless mazes of crumbling trenches and shell-torn tracks. Our objective was "Skyline Trench." I don't think, however, we ever reached it. A few hundred yards short we came across a dead man lying over the lip of the trench we were in, and looking over we saw several prostrate figures lying out in the open beyond. "Perhaps they are not *all* dead," one of the gunners remarked, and so we went over to see. Shells were beginning to drop around us, and how well I remember running up that sloping field and stooping over those lifeless bodies to see if any perchance still lived. One particularly clings to my mind, a lad, rigid, kneeling on one knee, with his head thrown forward, and his rifle still in his hand. He showed no signs of life, and I passed on. Leading up to "Skyline Trench," which ran along the summit of the ridge, was a shallow ditch. Here we found at length what we were looking for. There were several wounded lying in it, and I pounced on the first I saw—anxious, I must confess, to get away as quickly as I could—dressed his wound—it was in the stomach—as best I could, and as soon as the gunners whom we had sent back to the trench for the stretchers came along, I and the gunner with me got the wounded man on to a stretcher and started off. Meanwhile, the others had divided themselves into three parties of two each, leaving two men to act as reliefs, and these parties, each with a loaded stretcher, were soon following me back. Never till now did I realise how hard it is to carry a stretcher any distance over broken ground, especially if one has no slings. The journey back to Ovillers, sometimes in trenches, sometimes in the open, seemed absolutely interminable. Every moment I thought I should have to give in, and at each resting-place, every ten or twelve yards or so, we seemed to have laid our burden next to some monstrous heap of corpses. Never, even at Cambrai, did I see so many dead. At length we reached an old light railway—recently put in repair—which ran into the village, and here we ultimately laid our wounded in little trucks, which we pushed up to the Bearer-Post. Before we left him the man, the gunner and I had carried, was profuse in his thanks, in spite of the jolts and falls and wearisome slowness of the long carry. He was in the 1/5 Berks.

On 16th August the Battalion was withdrawn to billets at Bouzincourt. I joined them there and remained with them till Saturday, when they went into the line again, and I went to " details " at the Transport Lines. On the following evening as the Transport men were enjoying themselves over a game of football, the enemy started to shell the " lines." The horses were immediately set free and encouraged to scatter. The game continued as before, till things grew altogether so unpleasant that, like their horses, the players scattered too. I remembered how ridiculous our battalion goat looked, trotting along amongst the men and animals in an aimless, mystified sort of way. The next day we moved the " lines " to a safer spot on the western side of Bouzincourt.

On 21st August the Battalion was engaged in further active fighting. From the hill where our camp lay, Major M·T and I had a wonderful view of

1

the battle. When we got back he found an urgent note summoning him up to the Battalion at once. Next morning I went up myself to Battalion Headquarters, and, though our casualties had been heavy, and present discomfort extreme, I found everyone in the best of spirits. Major M'F—— was in charge of a forward headquarters, and it seemed communication with him was difficult, as his written messages were illegible and his voice on the 'phone impossible to hear. One urgent appeal for food was, however, deciphered and dealt with by the despatch of a cake and a bottle of port, on which the forward party breakfasted, lunched, and dined. In spite, however, of such minor difficulties, everything was going extremely well.

That night when I got back to camp I was almost entirely deserted, for about 9 P.M. orders were received for the sole remaining officer and all other personnel, including all the Pioneers, to proceed immediately up the line. I was left alone with the Transport Section. Happily, this did not last long, as the whole Battalion was withdrawn to Bouzincourt the following day, Wednesday, 23rd August.

We stayed in the village till Saturday, and then went to Forceville. From here our Brigade was detailed to occupy the trenches in front of Auchonvillers and facing Beaumont Hamel. On Sunday morning I said Mass in the village church, the only one which I ever found had been turned into a dressing-room and waiting-room for wounded. On Sunday, however, the authorities had no objection to its being put to its original purpose. That evening we went into the line. This was the first occasion on which I actually lived in the trenches. I had rather a dilapidated and distinctly unsafe little shanty to live in, just outside the mess. It was roofed with corrugated iron, the sides were of damp clay, where the shelter had been dug in, and the furniture consisted of a stretcher, one or two " ration " boxes, and some damp sand-bags. Not a very comfortable place, but I was far happier living with the Battalion than in exile at " details." Our mess-room was a cosy little place, with a snug little room adjoining, where the colonel and major lived, and the line on the whole was not too bad.

The most striking thing that occurred, during the ten days we spent in these parts, was an attack made on the stronghold of Thiepval on Sunday, 3rd September. We were not engaged in the actual attack. Our rôle was simply to " demonstrate " by rapid rifle and machine-gun fire, with the purpose of diverting the enemy's attention and drawing his fire. Just above our mess was an excellent observation post cut out of the side of the trench, and commanding a good view of the country to the south. The attack was timed to start at 3 A.M. We were all sitting up in the mess, including the O.C. of the 7th Worcesters who had come over from the left sector, when the Colonel said : " It's nearly three ; we'd better get out on top." It was pitch dark outside, and we had barely emerged from the mess and climbed out into the O.P. when suddenly— like some war scene in Olympia—the inky blackness was rent by the flashes of thousands of guns and the glare of innumerable lights, and the stillness of the night was torn asunder by a roaring tornado of sound.   It was one of the most weird and impressive sights I had ever seen.   And then, as the first faint streaks of dawn began to appear, we heard overhead the buzz of a fleet of aeroplanes, off to establish communication with the infantry, and all the while the rattle of our machine guns played an uninterrupted accompaniment to the general uproar.

As it grew light our own little coign of vantage showed signs of becoming unpleasant.   Several of our own shells, falling short, dropped in our lines just in front of us, happily without causing any casualties, and enemy machine guns began to sweep our own parapet.   I was standing next to the Adjutant when suddenly I felt an enormous thump on my left shoulder.   I turned round, thinking he was playing a joke on me, but found him engaged like the others in watching the scene before us as it unfolded itself in the early morning light.   I thought no more of it till, a few minutes later, he turned round towards me, and exclaimed, " Hullo, have you seen your star; it's got a hole right through it," referring to the metal star on my shoulder-strap. Further investigation showed another hole in the back of my tunic by my shoulder.   Then my shoulder began to feel a bit stiff and sticky behind, and taking off my coat, I found that a bullet had just grazed my shoulder, breaking the skin and causing it to bleed slightly.   The Doctor soon patched it up, and later in the morning I walked out through the communication trenches and over the open fields to say Mass, as I had arranged, in Mailly-Maillet church.

The following Wednesday we were relieved and went to Bus, and I remember how much I appreciated

the clean little room and bed I had there in the
Curé's house, after so many weeks of discomfort.
We remained at Bus just a week, and on 13th
September moved to Amplier near Doullens. Starting after the Battalion, another officer and myself
rode there by ourselves, making our way mostly
through some beautiful woods which bordered the
road. At Amplier we found the billets allotted us
—chiefly wooden huts—were in such a dirty condition that the Colonel got the Division Commander's
consent to move back to Sarton, which we did that
same night, and established ourselves there very
comfortably.

On a day of pouring rain, Monday the 18th, we
left Sarton, and skirting Doullens, marched to Boisbergues, which was to be our destination for some
days. As usual, whilst we were here I used to ride
round to the other battalions at Autheux, Le Meillard,
and Outrebois, getting at the same time several quiet
evening rides over lovely fields and woods.

We left Boisbergues for Sus-St-Leger, and hoping
to remain here a few days I fixed up Mass for the
following morning, which was Sunday. I was about
to begin when some of the men just coming in, told
me we were moving that morning. I said Mass for
the few that were already there, and returning to
the mess afterwards found everything packed up and
the Battalion preparing to start. I got breakfast, I
remember, from the people of the house, who were
extremely kind, and then R—— and I went round
the village to get all the billeting certificates from
houses where our men and officers had been lodged.
We then rode on after the Battalion, stopping for

lunch in the pretty village of Lucheux, and finally overtook the others, just as they were marching into Halloy.

We remained here one night, marched off next day to St Amand, only to return to Halloy the following day, 4th October. This time we remained here till the 10th.

Two nights before we left, I got a message from my old friend of the Ambulance, Lieut. M.——, now in the 3rd Division, to say that my brother was at Arqueves. Accordingly I rode over next morning to meet him, and found him with his battalion, the 2nd Suffolks, just preparing to go up the line, so that I had only a few minutes with him. This was the first and only time I saw him in France, for he was killed about a month later in an attack on Serre. I discovered also another brother of mine in the village, a chaplain with the 7th Field Ambulance, and I spent the afternoon with him. When I got back to Halloy I found we were to move next day to Humbercourt. Here one of our own officers was acting as Town Major. He was a wonderful musician, and came in to play for us one night after dinner. I remember also coming across a squadron of the North Irish Horse here. They . seemed a magnificent body of men and wonderfully turned out.

We stayed at Humbercourt three nights and then moved up to St Amand. On arriving here a room with three beds was allotted to the Adjutant, Doctor, and myself. The Adjutant and I coming in first chose the two canvas beds, leaving quite a good ordinary French bed for the Doctor. When the latter came in he was considerably annoyed, declaring we had chosen the best beds, and that his own was not strong enough to bear him. After thumping it about in various places to test its strength, he finally sat down violently in the centre of it, when to his horror and our own amusement, the bed subsided in the centre and folded over him. The bed was a collapsible one, and the catch had not been fastened

All this time a great scheme was on foot for an attack on Gommecourt. Everything had been planned out, including the exact rôle of each of our three brigades, and the number and function of the tanks allotted us The first inkling we had of the whole thing being cancelled was our Brigadier going on leave, followed a few days later by our Colonel too.

On Monday, the 16th, we went up to hold the line between Foncquevillers and Hebuterne, with Battalion Headquarters in the former village, three companies in the line and one at Hebuterne. Our mess was in a little wooden hut near my old chapel, and I slept in a tiny room with the Doctor, off one of the company messes near by. The good old Doctor had rather a habit of upsetting and disarranging things, and I remember my exasperation, one pouring wet night, when he came in after I had gone to bed and hung his dripping mackintosh over my shirt, and dropped my strop into the washing water. However, my last stay at Foncquevillers was really a very pleasant one. We could now in safety—it had been impossible before—go right along the trenches to Hebuterne, where one Company had its headquarters in a ruined house

On Thursday evening we left "Foncquy," as it

was familiarly called, riding back in the moonlight, Major M'F——, the Adjutant and Doctor, another officer and myself clattering down the frost-bound road to Souastre, and then turning north to St Amand.

Next morning, Friday, 20th October, we marched off to Sus-St-Leger, and remained here till the following Wednesday. The 1/4 Gloucesters were with us in the village The two other battalions were at Ivergny and Beaudricourt, both of which I naturally visited. On the evening before we left I took a solitary ride through the beautiful Lucheux woods, rich now with autumn tints, and supremely peaceful and quiet. I knew we were bound once more for the Somme.

(2) *Winter.*

On Wednesday, 26th October, we left Sus-St-Leger. We were to travel south in buses. To embus three or four battalions is always a difficult operation— there are never sufficient buses for one thing, just as there are never sufficient coaches on a troop train —and on this occasion confusion became more confounded by the sudden appearance of the French authorities, whose buses we were using, and who proceeded to take things into their own hands. After considerable confusion we were all securely packed in at last, and started off.

We got out a few miles west of Albert, on the Amiens road, and marched to billets in the little village of Bresle, where we met the Colonel just back from leave. Here we stayed, sending up recon-

noitring parties once or twice to the line, till
Tuesday, the 31st.

From Bresle we marched into Albert, and spent
Tuesday night there in very comfortable quarters
The following evening the Battalion moved up into
the line, and I remained with the "details" at Albert,
in a big empty house. On 4th November, after
having previously reconnoitred the ground with Lieut.
F—— as far up as Martinpuich, where the Battalion
then was, I left Albert and went up to live at the
A.D.S. which one of our Ambulances had opened
in the ruins of this village. The five days I spent at
Martinpuich have left with me some of the most last-
ing impressions of the whole war. The surrounding
country, on these black November days, was un-
speakably desolate. Martinpuich itself was nothing
but a heap of ruins lying mostly in a little valley of
its own, but with its western end on some slightly
rising ground which was crowned by the ruins of the
church. When we first arrived the road through
the village was scarcely distinguishable from the
surrounding débris. All around lay literally an
abomination of desolation. Behind us, a rising slope,
torn up by shell-holes, filled each with a filthy slimy
fluid, sometimes green, often red, strands of broken
wire everywhere, and twisted iron and endless mud,
and isolated graves. In front the village road
stretched out up the valley—"Death Valley" it was
called—towards Eaucourt l'Abbaye, Warlencourt
and Bapaume, and on either side the same dreary
vision of muddy wastes.

I slept in an old cellar—about a hundred yards
away from the deep dug-out where most of the

K

personnel lived—adjoining the actual Dressing Station, where there was always one medical officer and three or four orderlies on duty. The wounded used to be carried from here on stretchers to the light railway, which started near the dug-out and ran up the ridge and over the skyline, dipping down into the main Dressing Station at Contalmaison on the other side.

One dark winter's morning the O.C. of the Dressing Station and I sallied forth to reconnoitre a farm on the main Albert-Bapaume road, just behind the village of Le Sars. It was a place of evil repute and constantly shelled, and we had chosen what we fancied would be the quietest time to visit it. The idea was to establish if possible an A.D.S. or at any rate a bearer-post there. It was still quite dark when we reached the barricade which crossed the road behind Le Sars, so we sat there and waited for the dawn. A mystified machine-gun officer came stumbling up the road, and seeing nothing but two dim figures, wanted to know who the —— we were and what we were doing. On being told our purpose he muttered something about a "mad scheme" and passed on his way. As it grew lighter we made our way over to the ruined farm and set about looking for cellar accommodation, with the aid of a flash-lamp. We were soon interrupted by the disconcerting advent of several shells round the building The Doctor continued for a few minutes his cursory inspection, and then exclaimed—it was what I had been impatiently awaiting—that the place seemed no use, and that we had better make for home, which we did accordingly, as quickly as we could.

I was constantly meeting men of my own Battalion, either coming down wounded or passing through the village, and once when they were lying round Le Sars I paid them a brief early morning visit. In the afternoons I used to help in building up or extending our premises, and of an evening, when things were quiet, I would sit with the Doctor in my cellar and pay piquet. I also opened a new cemetery whilst I was here, on the slope of the hill leading back towards Contalmaison. It started with a single lonely grave, but grew bigger day by day till, when I left, it was quite a conspicuous landmark.

On the Sunday after I arrived at Martinpuich a big attack was launched on the famous Butte de Warlencourt, though our Division was not actually engaged. The entire Butte was captured in a few minutes at the point of the bayonet, but the enfilade fire from the trenches south-west of it, which the enemy still held, was so severe that it had to be relinquished that same day; and it remained henceforth a constant eyesore to Divisional and Corps commanders who were repeatedly planning its reduction.

The Battalion was relieved on the 8th November, and on the 9th I rejoined them at Contalmaison Camp, just behind where the village of that name once stood. Battalion Headquarters was in a large deep old German dug-out At the foot of the main entrance there was a little room on the left which served as mess, and also as the Colonel's bedroom. To the right lay a long gallery full of two tiers of beds where we others and some of the company officers used to sleep, and beyond that, with another shaft leading out, was the Orderly Room The

weather was constantly cold, misty, and wet, but with
the aid of a stove we made ourselves extremely cosy
inside ; and, in fact, sometimes we were almost too
warm. We stayed here ten days. On Sundays I
used to say Mass in a little hut on the far side of
the valley across the Fricourt road, near the camps of
the 4th Gloucesters and 7th Worcesters. The 8th
Worcesters were beside us. Often I used to walk over
to Fricourt and Becourt, and sometimes as far as
Albert, passing on the way the famous craters of La
Boiselle. One afternoon I walked over with R——
to Ovillers, to locate if possible the graves of some of
our men. On the way, in a little gully in the old
German front line, we came across the dead body of
a German. He must have been lying there since 1st
July, and yet he seemed to be in an extraordinary
good state of preservation. Ovillers we found vastly
changed from what it had been when we left it in
August. A fine metalled road now ran right through
the village, and up towards what once had been
"Skyline Trench," and there was a constant stream
of lorries, wagons, and ammunition limbers going up
and down, feeding the big guns which lay ensconced
on all sides. We failed to find the graves we were
looking for, and after wandering up and down our
own old trenches, to the accompaniment of occasional
shells from Thiepval, we returned home.

On Monday, the 20th, we went into the line again
beyond Martinpuich. This time, instead of going to
the A.D.S., I went up with the Battalion. When we
reached Brigade Headquarters in Martinpuich the
Colonel went in for a few minutes to see the General,
the Adjutant and I waiting outside. As we started

off again the enemy put some heavy shells right up on the higher part of the village behind us. We turned to watch them bursting, thinking ourselves at a safe distance, when an enormous fragment came hurtling past us, burying itself at our feet, so we pressed on over open country to the line, the Colonel leading.

We reached our dug-out in safety. We were relieving the 7th Worcesters, and my first duty on arriving was to bury—with the aid of a flash-lamp, for it was now quite dark—one of their men who had been killed that afternoon. We buried him in the field just behind the Headquarters.

Our party here was quite a small one, consisting of the Colonel and Adjutant, K—— R——, and myself We made ourselves as comfortable as could be under the circumstances, but the dug-out persisted in having such an unpleasant smell about it that we all set to work one afternoon to clear it out. This was not easy, as everything had to be carried out up a flight of some thirty steps. We found the floor of the dug-out to be almost two inches deep in compressed mud and filth of every description. I don't suppose it had ever been cleaned out since the Germans had first built it. The five of us, however, went hard to work, and eventually we got it more or less clean. Two further rooms opened out of the one we used. The first was allotted to our servants, who cooked and slept there; the one beyond was used by the Signallers and other Headquarter personnel. I used often to issue out the rum to these men in the evening, and I suppose I was unusually generous in my allowance for one night I heard a man say "Oh! I'm not going to bother about it";

to which another replied, " But do you know who is issuing it ? " Our own mess continued to be extraordinarily good, in spite of the distance it was to bring stuff up.

Of the companies, one lay just behind our Headquarters, one occupied a trench a few hundred yards in front, and two were in the front line right up against the Butte de Warlencourt, with their joint Headquarters and the Aid Post, where the Doctor lived, in a dug-out a little way behind in a sunken road. The walk up to them was by no means a pleasant one. There were two routes, one straight overland to the support trench, then to the " Mill," a prominent mound beyond, and thence by a shallow trench up to the sunken road. The whole way, till one dipped into dead ground on approaching the road, one was under full observation from the Butte. The other way consisted of turning to the left on leaving our dug-out and cutting into the road out of Martinpuich village at a point known as " Dead Mule Corner," crossing the road, and then bearing to the right up the valley till one struck the sunken road again and turned right to get to the company Headquarters It was a longer way, but enjoyed the reputation, quite unfounded I fancy, of being safer.

My first walk overland I took with R——, a wild spirit who delighted in running risks, and yet whose presence inspired confidence. Our walk on this occasion was moderately untroubled, except for a sniper who worried us on the way back ; but on another occasion, when the Adjutant was with us as well, we got nastily chased by whizz-bangs between the " Mill " and the support trench

Everywhere the dead were lying about in large numbers, but any organised attempt at burial was rendered difficult by hostile shelling. In front of our Battalion Headquarters, which was on the site of an old German gun position, was a sunken road with a bank and a hedge on the far side. Here, fairly sheltered and concealed, one had a good view of the surrounding country. I often looked out over a stretch of broken ground towards the little wood which marked Eaucourt l'Abbaye. One day, looking over the familiar view with glasses, I discovered to my horror that the little rising mounds scattered broadcast over the fields were the khaki-covered, mud-stained remnants of dead soldiers. The company in support managed to bury several, and others, of course, had already done their share before us. I remember in particular one white wooden cross which stood up prominently on the further slope of "Death Valley."

On the 23rd November we were relieved. Just as it was getting dusk K—— and I started to walk back to the camp allotted us near Bazentin. Before we got anywhere near the camp, however, it was pitch dark, and it was only after considerable difficulty that we ultimately found our way at all, stumbling all the while over trenches and shell-holes. My electric torch, of course, refused to function just when we most needed it.

As a camp Bazentin was a complete failure, and heavy rains had reduced it to a mere swamp. The men, after all the hardships of the line, were housed in miserable shelters of earth and wood, though we at Battalion Headquarters had the comparative luxury

of a wood and canvas hut.   The camp was, moreover, away from any good road, and barely accessible
even in daylight.   K——— and I settled ourselves in
the hut, and awaited the arrival of the others.   They
turned up in the small hours of the morning, having
lost their way ; but the Colonel was still as cheery as
ever in spite of the discomfort and cold and wet.   He
was most amusing at nights, saying, as he wrapped
himself up in innumerable woolly waistcoats, that
instead of undressing one had to dress for bed.   To
add to our discomforts the camp was intermittently
shelled, and I remember one night the ridiculous
appearance we all presented sitting up in our valises,
some with tin hats on, listening to the shells which
seemed to burst nearer and nearer, scattering fragments of mud and muck on to the delicate canvas
roof of our hut.   The Sunday we spent here was the
only one in my recollection when I absolutely gave
up in despair any attempt to say Mass for the men.
I had spent the greater part of Saturday trudging in
the rain over the vast expanses of mud which lay all
round our brigade camps looking in vain for some
suitable place, and I came home at last as it was
growing dark, wet, tired, and with nothing arranged.

The state of our camp and the extreme discomfort
of the men induced the Colonel to take active steps
to have us moved, and he adopted one very cunning
ruse to demonstrate to the Divisional Staff the
conditions under which we lived.   He induced one
of them, whom he had met in the afternoon, to stay
and have tea with us, and kept him till it was quite
dark.   The Staff Officer at length got up to go, and
the Colonel took him to the door, and opening it,

disclosed the inky blackness without   He implored us to lend him a torch—we had none—and after being vaguely pointed out the direction in which he wanted to go, we watched him grope his way painfully along with the aid of a flickering stump of candle, and finally disappear in the darkness.

Next day we moved to another camp, unfurnished, it is true, but still providing ample accommodation in Nissen huts for both men and officers.   The Pioneers immediately started to build us a good Battalion Headquarters, and, as the Colonel put it, we sat in a field whilst our house grew up around us.

On Friday, 1st December, the Battalion moved up again into the line.   This time we were to be in support, a little behind where we were before, with Battalion Headquarters at a place called "Seven Elms."   There was a thick mist when the Adjutant, the Doctor, and I set out for our new quarters N—— was to show us the way, and for the first hour or so all went well, and then the mist seemed to gather round us more heavily and shroud us in more deeply, and still the duck-board track led on and on, and still we followed it.   At length we came to a sunken road.   Where were we?   None of us had the slightest idea.   A few shells dropping unpleasantly near us warned us we were approaching the line.   Should we turn left, or right, or push straight on?   As we were debating what to do we saw some men and asked them the way to Martinpuich.   To my surprise they told us to turn to the right, and then I suddenly made out in the mist a row of big guns and some tanks, and knew we were in the sunken road leading out of Martinpuich village on to the

Albert road.   I could only explain how we got there by supposing that where another track coming up from the right crossed ours at a very broad angle we must have inadvertently borne to the left instead of carrying straight on.   When we got back to Martinpuich, however, we soon got our bearings again, and finally reached " Seven Elms " with little further difficulty.

We stayed here five days, with one company in the village, and the other three manning a trench which ran roughly south-east from Martinpuich towards our Headquarters.   Visiting the companies by day was easy enough, though one frequently had to edge off to a flank to avoid hostile shelling, especially on fine days when observation was good. Battalion Headquarters in a deep dug-out and the Company in the village were comfortable enough, but the other three had to make the best of what little accommodation they could find in the trenches. These were certainly very bad and muddy, and there was no possibility of getting them dry till the weather mended.   On our right, conditions were even worse, and I remember hearing of a man there who had sunk up to the armpits in mud, and whose rescue caused considerable difficulty.

Our own Battalion Headquarters were distinctly cosy and warm, though a trifle crowded, as the officers of one of the companies lived with us.   I used to sleep on a stretcher on the mess-room floor with K—— on a stretcher on the table above me. However, the more we were the warmer we were, and we had altogether a very pleasant, cheery time.

On the 5th we went back to Shelter-Wood Camp,

almost opposite our old Contalmaison Camp, and overlooking the valley and a little wood from which the camp got its name. We were fairly comfortable here, men and officers alike in Nissen huts, which though sometimes cold and draughty, had always the advantage of being dry, no matter how bad the weather.

Whilst we were here Colonel M—— left us to take command temporarily of an army school, and the adjutant's brother, Major W. N——, came up from a course he had been on, to take over command. The Somme had proved too strenuous for a man of Major M'F——'s years, and he had left us some weeks back. On 8th December, the Feast of the Immaculate Conception, I managed to say Mass for as many of my men as I could get together in a big marquee which was used for concerts. On Saturday we went into the line again.

This time it was our turn for the front line, and we occupied once more the trenches and dug-outs facing the Butte de Warlencourt, into which we had gone originally. Here life was much as it had been previously I remember spending one morning burying the dead with the aid of some Ambulance men, and, one afternoon, assembling with the others to watch an hour's bombardment of the Butte, much in the same spirit as one might have gone to the "Empire" just to see a "show." The Butte used to stand out prominently in white chalk—a landmark for miles around, with the dark masses of Loupart Wood behind—and it was quite amusing to watch large masses of it being removed by our bursting shells; but I don't suppose much harm was done to

those who lived in deep dug-outs beneath.   It seemed
a sort of obsession with generals that the Butte
should be captured, and a brief spell of fine weather
suddenly brought things to a climax.   Our Division
was ordered to attack it, and the preceding night
"Death Valley" and the sunken road at the end of
it was a seething mass of men carrying up ammunition, wiring stakes, bombs, water, and "Very" lights.
I guided Major N——— up that night to the forward
companies.   It was a miracle that the enemy did not
shell us.   In the midst of all this feverish activity
the weather broke, and the attack was cancelled.

The following night, Tuesday, the 12th, we were
relieved and went back to "Seven Elms."   The
distance could not have been more than five hundred
yards, and yet I spent nearly two hours in getting back.
All through Tuesday afternoon and evening the
enemy had been harassing the ground all round our
Battalion Headquarters with bursts of rapid shell-fire.
I was going to walk back with the Adjutant who had
been rather seedy during the last few days.   We
had barely emerged from the trench into the open
ground above our dug-out when the enemy opened
fire.   We had to rush for cover into the nearest
shell-hole, and there we lay cowering for several
minutes with shells bursting all round us.   One
flashed up barely two yards from us and covered us
with débris, but being below the level of the ground
we luckily escaped ; but thinking the next one might
possibly land in our own shell-hole, we crawled out
and got quickly into the cover afforded by an old
trench.   It was a most unpleasant time.   I remember
hearing a voice crying out in the darkness to know

the way back, then I saw the man's figure standing out in the glare of a distant "Very" light, then came a sudden crash of shells, followed by an unearthly stillness. When things seemed to have quietened down somewhat, N—— and I emerged from the trench and made our way in the direction, as I thought, of "Seven Elms." We wandered on, N—— stumbling a lot and falling from time to time, so that I began to be afraid he might collapse altogether. After vainly endeavouring to find our direction, I saw a light in the distance and we made for that. I found it to be a post occupied by men of the Division on our right. We learnt the way back from them, and finally arrived in safety at the dug-out at Seven Elms.

We only stayed here two nights, and on Thursday, the 14th, we went back to the same area around Contalmaison. This time we went under canvas at "Shelter-Wood Camp, North." After two nights here the Division was relieved, but our Brigade was detailed to remain for road making and repairing, the other two Brigades having already done their share of this work before the division went into the line. In consequence, on Saturday, the 16th, we vacated "Shelter-Wood Camp, North," for the incoming Division, and trudged over in the mud to another camp—tents again—on the edge of Mametz Wood. This was another period of the war destined to linger long in my memory. It was a time in which extreme physical discomfort was not merely made bearable but quite counterbalanced by the pleasure derived from the company of those with whom one lived. For me there was actually

very little to do. For the first week it was almost
impossible to leave the camp and regain the road
without sinking knee-deep in mud, and I used—
when I wanted to spend a quiet half-hour by myself
—to wander out into Mametz Wood, with its gaunt,
shrivelled trees and bare branches and lonely graves
and litter of war. Sometimes I would wander
further afield, and two or three times some of us
rode into Albert and lunched at the excellent officers'
café there. When I think of the Somme there rises
always to my mind the vision of the bleak muddy
road which stretched out north-east from Albert,
rising over the ridge and then dipping down to
La Boiselle, forking there, one arm going straight
forward to Pozieres, the other bending round to
Contalmaison, and of the eternal limbers moving
slowly up and down with the drivers lolling in their
saddles, and the deep collars of their coats turned up
over their ears, and of every now and then a group of
infantry plodding wearily along, and a lorry or car
overtaking the slower traffic and splashing everyone
with mud.

Whilst we were at Mametz Wood, I went to visit
my brother who was then at Louvencourt with the
7th Field Ambulance. I first rode down to Albert
and stayed the night with our Transport Officer who
had his horse lines there. Next morning, after an
early breakfast, I rode off over the slippery ice-bound
roads to Louvencourt. I got there without mishap,
though my orderly's horse slipped right down,
luckily without hurting himself or the rider. I had
lunch with my brother and spent a few very pleasant
hours with him, and he rode back with me as far

as Acheux. There we parted, and I rode on to Albert, and thence made my way to Mametz Wood, getting a lift in a lorry to La Boiselle and walking on from there.

The frost, by drying up the ground, had improved our camp a lot, and a few days before we left, we were able to move our Headquarters into an old German dug-out just vacated by another unit. Here we were quite comfortable, and the change from an icy tent into a warm dug-out was most welcome A canteen also was set up in a marquee at the bottom of the valley which ran down by the side of the wood, and on Sunday I used it for Mass. Unfortunately, it was shortly afterwards demolished by one of the few shells which from time to time Fritz put over our camp.

On Christmas Day we were all busy moving, but I managed to say an early Mass in my old tent at which two or three contrived to be present, and then we marched off to another camp at Fricourt where we lodged in Nissen huts.

Here the Battalion had its Christmas dinner. Every man had his portion of turkey and plum pudding, supplemented, of course, by other things, and all were in excellent spirits.

The Major, with the Adjutant and myself, visited all the huts where the festivities were taking place, and in a short speech, wished the men a happy Christmas. In one hut after the usual "three cheers for the Major," a well-known character in the Battalion shouted out, much to my amusement, "and one for the clergyman," with the accent strong on the centre syllable

One night the Scotch officers, of whom we had several in the Battalion, gave a dinner to all the other officers. It was a genuine Scotch affair, including the haggis, introduced solemnly into the mess by two pipers, borrowed from a neighbouring Scotch unit, who continued to play throughout the meal. Unfortunately, towards the end of the proceedings, they gradually succumbed to the generous draughts of drink, provided to sustain them in their musical efforts, with the result that the Scotch "lament," which was to be the final item in their programme, sounded, not merely to the uninitiated like myself, but to the native Scotch as well, a mere medley of discordant sounds.

On Friday we left for Becourt Camp, one of the most comfortable we had been in so far. Becourt village was completely in ruins, but I remember the district on account of the pretty surrounding woods and the beautifully situated British cemetery which lies in their midst by the roadside.

On the following day Saturday, 30th December, we marched back into civilisation once more and billeted at Contay. On the way, from the high ground above Albert, I had my last view of that vast expanse of horse lines and camps which lay on the sloping ground east of the city, with Aveluy church spire and the flooded Ancre in the far distance towards the north.

CHAPTER V

WE arrived at Contay on 30th December 1916. Most of us at Headquarters were billeted in the Curé's house, and we had our mess there also. The 4th Gloucesters were at Contay with us, and the Worcesters a few miles away, each in a separate village. In my rides round the country I came across some cavalry not far away. I forget their regiment, but I remember some of them joining my slender congregation at Contay church. I also paid one or two visits to our artillery, and said Mass for them one Sunday. At Contay there was a Casualty Clearing Station, with its usual accompaniment, a big military cemetery, covering nearly an acre of ground, with its long rows of wooden crosses, standing out in exact alignment like some perfectly drilled battalion, motionless on parade.

In the early hours of Monday morning, 8th January, we marched away to Heilly and entrained there about half-past eight. After the usual railway journey on a French troop train, we detrained about four hours later at Pont Remy, and marched off towards Huppy. Colonel H—— of the Worcesters, temporarily commanding the Brigade, had the happy

M

notion of providing the men, cold and stiff after
the journey, with hot coffee, and various estaminets
were requisitioned in the village near the station
to get it ready. I think most of the men got their
coffee, but unfortunately the weather was blowing
up for rain and sleet, and the coffee-drinking delayed
us considerably. At length, however, we formed
up and started off again. A few minutes later,
down came the rain, icy cold, and it continued
blowing a regular blizzard all through the weary
miles towards Huppy. As we mounted the high
ground on which the village lay, the cold became
more intense than ever, and, though walking briskly
one's hands became absolutely stiff and numb. It
was with real relief that we stumbled finally into the
village. The billets here were very good. Battalion
Headquarters was in a chateau, with a good room
for each officer, all steam-heated, a mess-room and
anteroom, and, luxury of luxuries, a bathroom with
hot water laid on.

The village church was a large and really handsome one. The week-day Mass was said in the
transept—which formed a sort of little chapel in
itself, and was more easily heated than the main
body of the church—and I was most impressed by
the custom which prevailed here of the congregation
answering the responses in a body, and joining with
the priest in saying the " Gloria " and " Credo." Early
morning Mass used to be a most touching and
devotional ceremony. The priest here had originally
been Curé at Thiepval, but had managed, since the
war, to make his way back into France via Holland
and England. He told me he was in Thiepval

when the French had attacked it early in the
war, and that if only they had pressed their attack
the least bit more the place would have been won,
as the enemy had already begun to evacuate it.

The other Battalions of the Brigade were as usual
scattered in various other villages round about, and
my work naturally took me to visit them, and, as
far as possible, arrange Mass for them. Consequently
I enjoyed several very pleasant country rides during
my stay here.

On the afternoon of Sunday, the 14th, I rode
down to Abbeville, took the train there for Amiens,
and so via Havre to England on my second
" leave."

I got back to the Battalion on Thursday night,
1st February, after spending some of the coldest
hours of my life wandering over the country-side
in a motor lorry, which finally deposited me at
about half-past ten at Cappy on the Somme. I
found the Battalion was in a camp near by, known
as Camp 56, on the Eclusier road, and set out to
find it. Luckily I met one of our officers coming
back from a reconnoitring expedition, and he showed
me the way in. It was nearly midnight when I
at length made my way into the Headquarter officers'
hut, and in spite of their being thus rudely awakened,
I found them all as cheery as ever. After a brief
meal, I too soon settled myself to sleep.

Next day we were to relieve a French battalion
in the line, and on Friday afternoon we marched
out from our camp. When we got near the line
we got off our horses, and the Major, Adjutant,
K——, and I walked on behind a French N.C.O.

who was acting as guide. After walking for about an hour through interminable communication trenches, we at length arrived at our destination, and were received with open arms by the French C.O. and his Second-in-command. They were the most cheery and amusing pair imaginable. After an excellent dinner, and some special wine produced in our honour, they regaled us with French songs, both comic and otherwise, till far on into the night, when they wrapped themselves up in their coats and bade us a tender farewell.

The line we were holding ran roughly between the villages of Biache and Barleux, with the Somme, in a deep valley, in front of us, and Peronne on the farther bank. On our left loomed out the menacing masses of Mont St Quentin. For the first day or two we were covered by French guns and had a French officer living with us. We were, moreover, on the extreme right of the British line, so that the Battalion next us was French. On the morning after we had arrived the Adjutant and I went to visit their Regimental Headquarters, and were most courteously received. We found the Regimental Commander in a state of almost complete undress, having his hair cut, and so his Second-in-command did most of the talking, the C.O. throwing in a comment from time to time. We left them with mutual expressions of goodwill.

The line we were holding was, during our first trip, extremely dry. The hard frosts of the preceding days had so bound up the clayey soil that the sides of the trenches were like cliffs of granite, and a shell bursting amongst them would dislodge great boulders hard as rocks, and impossible to clear away. On Sunday night, 14th February, the enemy put down a heavy barrage on our front and support lines, and raided us. He cunningly chose as his point of entry the exact junction of the French and British lines, but as soon as he entered instead of turning left towards the extreme left French post, he turned right towards our extreme right post. The raid was "completely repulsed." This is an official phrase, and seeing every raiding party means ultimately to return to its own lines, is rather ambiguous. However, when a raiding party secures no prisoners or material, and though causing casualties, leaves dead and wounded in the enemies' lines, the phrase becomes literally true, as it was in this case. It was not, however, till all was over that we at Battalion Headquarters knew what had happened. As soon as the enemy barrage came down, the telephone wires, as invariably happens in such cases, were cut, and our first news was brought by a runner who tumbled breathless down into our dug-out, and gasped out that the Germans had attacked and were occupying our front line. We were all old enough soldiers to take his story with "a grain of salt." Two officers went up the line immediately and soon brought back the true story. We revived the runner who was naturally badly shaken, and soon afterwards a wounded German prisoner was brought in. We tried to revive him too, but with less success as he was badly wounded in the leg, and so, after getting from him his name and regiment, we sent him off with the stretcher-bearers to the A.D.S.

On Wednesday, the 9th we were relieved, and

made our way back—a long moonlight walk, I remember, over bleak, bare, frosty roads, and through ruined villages—to Marly Camp, which was on the farther side of Cappy and near the partially inhabited village of Chuignolles. We spent ten days here in huts, and in spite of the intense cold, were fairly comfortable. A large coal dump on the railway line which ran through our camp contributed, I fancy, in no small degree to the general warmth of the troops. I used to walk every morning, rubbing my frozen fingers, to say Mass at the village church at Chuignolles, and on Sunday I said Mass at Cappy. The walk from our camp to Cappy was a very pretty one. One could either go up the hill overlooking our camp, and then down again the other side into the village, or one could follow the road which ran round the hill, with the Somme canal on one side and a high almost perpendicular cliff on the other. This was the longer but more level road.

On Saturday, the 12th, we left Marly Camp and went up to occupy the trenches again. Whilst we were in the line the thaw came, and the trenches, from being hard and dry, were turned into unspeakable morasses of thick, sticky mud, so deep in places that men were constantly getting stuck fast in it, and had to be bodily dragged out from above. When walking round I used to tie a couple of sandbags above my trench boots, and in that way kept fairly dry, as the mud was not liquid enough to penetrate far or quickly.

During this tour in the line we attempted a small raid of our own. The intention was to surprise an advanced post and kill or capture the garrison. In

spite, however, of vast preparations, including that
of "bangalore torpedoes"—a patent wire-cutting
device—and the assembling in our dug-out of various
officers of artillery and from the Brigade, nothing
materialised, as on the night in question the post
was found to be unoccupied. Whilst, however, we
were still awaiting news of the raiding party, a wire
was handed to me, which ran : "You will proceed to
57th Division to take up duty as S.C.F. Non C. of E."
I was completely taken aback by this unexpected
order, and decided that under the circumstances I
could do nothing for the moment to comply with it.

On Thursday, the 22nd, we went into support, to a
line just behind the front system in a locality known
as "Achille Ravine." Here we had extremely
comfortable headquarters in a dug-out cut into the
side of the valley bank Three of the companies
were more or less similarly accommodated, and one
lived a little way back in cellars amidst the ruins of
Flaucourt. In the centre of "Achille Ravine" we
had buried those killed during our two tours in the
line, and before we left we railed off the little cemetery
where they all lay together, and erected a big white
cross, with their names on, to mark the spot.

On Saturday, 24th February, we returned to
Camp 56 by Cappy. I rode out early that afternoon
to arrange about Mass, and when I got back to camp
I found Doctor H——, who had been with us since
December, but had left us at Marly Camp to go on
leave. He had just got back, and whilst we were
waiting for the others to arrive, we went out together
to see our Divisional Concert Party, who were giving a
show that night in a camp adjoining ours. They were

always worth seeing, and did not, as is so often the case, cloak deficiency of talent by vulgarity and coarseness.

A day or so later, I saw for the first time an enemy aeroplane attacking one of 'our balloons. I was sitting in the mess about tea-time when I heard a lot of shouting outside, and, opening the door, saw a group of our men watching the fight. The aeroplane, completely indifferent apparently to the anti-aircraft shells bursting around it, was circling round the balloon and firing tracer bullets into it. Suddenly the balloon burst into flames and the aeroplane flew off unscathed. It was a very still evening, and as I watched the parachutes, in which the two observers had long since jumped out, descending slowly and vertically beneath the balloon, I saw to my horror that the balloon itself, falling in flames, was rapidly gaining on them. It was a race as to which should reach the ground first. From where we stood we could not see what ultimately happened, but we heard afterwards that one observer escaped unhurt, but that the other was so badly burnt that he subsequently died.

It was at Camp 56 on the banks of the Somme that I had at last, on Friday, 2nd March, to say good-bye to the 6th Gloucesters, with whom I had spent so many varied but constantly happy months. It was with real feelings of regret that I went round the camp for the last time, and there was but little pleasure in the long ride that afternoon down to the rail-head at Chuignes ; though luckily L. C. N—— the Adjutant, rode down with me and kept me company. The mess-cart followed us with my kit. We found that I had some time to wait at the station, so L. C., after waiting for the safe arrival of my luggage, said good-bye to me there, and I watched him riding away, till a bend in the road hid him from sight. Six weeks later he was dead, and all the Headquarter Officers I had known so well with him. They were killed by the explosion of a delayed-action German mine while sleeping in a cellar just vacated by the enemy in his great Somme Withdrawal.

For me a new chapter in the war was opening, and as on my first arrival, so now, it began with a long railway journey. The train was made up of French trucks all bearing the familiar label, "Hommes 40 Chevaux 8." I selected the cleanest I could find, and shortly before the train left I was joined by a Scotch officer from the 1st Black Watch. We started off in the usual leisurely way about four o'clock in the afternoon, Friday, 2nd March, and reached Amiens without incident, as the evening was closing in. Here we were joined by three French soldiers, and then we started off again. We had been moving slowly forward for about an hour, when, in a most bleak and lonely spot, with no house in view, we stopped. This was nothing out of the ordinary, but after waiting about half an hour we began to notice the delay and got out. The track here was on an evident incline, and it appeared that the engine, after struggling up as best it could, had at length given up the effort as beyond its powers, and we were now awaiting the arrival of another engine to help us. Meanwhile the cold was getting intense, and my canny Scot, after producing a batman from the remoter recesses of the train, proceeded with his help to improvise a fire The batman went off in search of fuel, whilst the officer, having borrowed his

Y

bayonet, punched holes in the side of an old bucket we found lying, by the track. The man, in spite of the apparent destitution of the neighbourhood, soon returned with large quantities of wood. We arranged some in the bucket, and by dint of vigorous swinging, soon got it well alight. We then built up a heap of sand—taken from the permanent way—in the middle of the floor of the truck, and when all was ready placed the flaming brazier on the top. We then closed the folding doors, and drawing up our valises sat and warmed ourselves by the fire, carrying on all the while a desultory conversation with our French friends and sharing with them our provisions of chocolate and biscuits. Ultimately—on the arrival, I suppose, of the second engine—we started to move again. Then I dozed off, and lying as low down as possible to avoid the dense smoke, which every addition of fuel produced from our brazier, I finally fell fast asleep.

I awoke several hours later, cold, stiff, and grimy. I got up and opened the doors of our truck. Dawn was just breaking, and looking back into the interior of the wagon, I saw that the three Frenchmen had left us during the night, and that I was alone with the Scotch officer. Presently, he too awoke, and together we stood looking out from the open doorway on to the dreary landscape. We came to a station—Abancourt—and stopped. The name left me unmoved. I had no notion where we were. Suddenly it dawned on me I had passed that station before when approaching Rouen on my last leave. Rouen—that was of no use to either of us: and yet that was where the train seemed bent on taking us,

and we both wanting all the time to get to Abbeville.
Assuring myself from a military policeman who was
standing on the platform that my fears were not
groundless, we both of us precipitated ourselves and
our belongings out of the train, just as it was moving
off. Its departure seemed to make the surrounding
emptiness more complete than ever. We found to
our joy, however, that Abancourt boasted a buffet
which in due course would open, and might be doubtless induced to provide breakfast. It did so, and an
excellent breakfast it was. Then after a prolonged
rest and a smoke we began once more to think of
renewing our journey. A diminutive but very
friendly R.T O. assured us that if we could only get
back to the next station—Romescamp—we should
find an abundance of trains all going to Abbeville
The question, however, was how to get there. For
ourselves we might easily walk—it was only a mile
or two up the line the R.T.O. told us, and he used
often to walk there for company—but how about our
valises. The R.T.O. hit on a solution. Trains for
Romescamp, it appeared, had a marked dislike to
stopping at Abancourt on the way, but he thought
he might induce one to stop if he tried. I must
admit he did his best nobly. Two trains came
through while we waited ready with our luggage;
but in spite of the R.T.O. running along by the
engine, imploring the drivers to stop, they remained
obdurate, and passed on in callous indifference to
his entreaties. Still somehow or other we must get
to Romescamp. The idea of remaining imprisoned
at Abancourt was intolerable. We issued out into
the straggling village—consisting solely of a few

isolated houses—in the hopes of raising some sort of
conveyance, or possibly jumping a lorry. A cab,
however, was obviously something unheard of, and
the road, even if it did lead to Romescamp—it showed
no signs of doing so from where we were—was
practically devoid of any traffic, except one or two
fleeting cars which flashed unheeding past us.
Suddenly, my Scotch friend had an idea. Opposite
the station was an estaminet—surely an estaminet was
not complete without a wheelbarrow of sorts—why
not hire a wheelbarrow, and possibly a boy to wheel it,
and get our kit along to Romescamp that way. We
entered the estaminet. A girl was behind the
counter and one man in front of it drinking. On
our entry the girl made a sudden dive under the
counter and produced a printed card which she held
up to us in silence. On it in bold, black letters was
printed, " Out of bounds to British troops." I said,
" No matter, we don't want a drink, we want to
borrow *une petite voiture*," and I explained our
purpose. In Tommy's parlance there was " nothing
doing," neither a drink which we didn't want nor a
barrow which we did. Disconsolate we returned to
the station. Here, however, good news awaited us.
It appeared a train was due shortly, which would stop
at Abancourt whether we wanted it to or not. In
time it did, and about midday we arrived at the Land
of Promise, Romescamp, with its innumerable sidings
and bustling activity and countless trains. We
hurried to the R.T.O.'s office, and found there not
one merely but three. When was the next train to
Abbeville, we inquired. None till to-morrow afternoon ; and so I was faced with another day to spend,

kicking my heels in a village which proved on investigation to be no larger and considerably dirtier than Abancourt.   My Scotch friend, however, was luckier than I, because it appeared there was a train which would take him direct to his destination that afternoon, and so we parted.   I had lunch and dinner in an estaminet set aside for officers, and spent a most uncomfortable night on the hard floor of the station waiting-room, which a kindly railway department had built specially for officers and tastefully furnished with one narrow wooden bench running round the walls.   Next morning I managed a wash at one of the men's "ablution benches," and had breakfast in the estaminet.   Later, I discovered my train, and after sitting in it for an hour or more we started at length for Abbeville   We arrived about eight that evening, and I got dinner and a bed in the hotel near the station.   Next morning, Monday, we renewed the journey, this time making for Etaples. I had met the previous day at Romescamp an officer who was bound for St Pol, and we had been travelling together.   I had only once been on this line before, and then it was by night, so that I was not well acquainted with it.   Neither apparently was my companion, for both of us failed to get out when the train stopped—nor indeed at Etaples station, but some way beyond it—and got carried off to Pont-de-Briques, near Boulogne.   Realising our mistake we got out here, and luckily, after waiting about some time, we found a goods train returning to Etaples. We boarded this, and ultimately—after an interminable piece of shunting at Le Touquet which nearly sent me crazy—we arrived at Etaples that evening.

Another day gone. We got an excellent dinner at the club and beds in a neighbouring hotel.

On Tuesday morning early, leaving my companion still in bed as his train did not leave till later, I got a train which deposited me at Hazebrouck at five o'clock in the evening. Here I spent another night, sleeping at the officers' rest-house, after having dined at an hotel in the town. Wednesday morning I was up early again and caught a train at 6.45 which brought me to my final destination, Steenwerck, an hour later. Steenwerck was then rail-head for the 57th Division, and having met an officer bound like myself for Divisional Headquarters at Sailly, we left our luggage at the station to be called for later, and started to walk. We had been assured we should pick up a lorry on the way, but none passed us, and so we covered the four or five miles on foot.

On reaching Sailly, I reported myself—long over-due—to Divisional Headquarters, and it was arranged that temporarily at any rate I should live there. A billet was soon found for me and my luggage sent for.

CHAPTER VI

SUMMER IN THE LINE

I HAD arrived at Sailly on Wednesday, 9th March, and after living a few days with D mess of Division, I was attached to the 2/4 South Lancs. and moved up to Armentières, where their quartermaster stores were, and got a billet in the Rue Sadi Carnot. By Sunday, the 18th, however, I was transferred to the 2/5 South Lancs. to whom I ought originally to have gone, and I moved in consequence to Rue Marle, a suburb of Armentières. Here I messed with Battalion Headquarters at Crown Prince House, and had a billet in the Curé's house. When my own Battalion went into the line, and the 2/4 South Lancs. took its place at Rue Marle, through the courtesy of this latter Battalion I continued to mess at "Crown Prince" House.

I had hardly settled down to my new surroundings and paid one or two visits to the trenches—including, on a very wet and cold morning, a visit for a funeral at a spot known as Ration Farm Cemetery—when the whole Brigade was withdrawn into rest billets between Erquinghem and Bac St Maur. The 2/5 South Lancs. had their billets in Rue Dormoir, a country lane running off the main road. Battalion

Headquarters was in a fine old moated farm, and the Signalling Officer and I shared a room in a clean little cottage near Fort Rompu. The other Battalions of the Brigade were the 2/10 Liverpool Scottish who were at Bac St Maur, the 2/9 King's Liverpool Regiment at Erquinghem, and the 2/4 South Lancs. who were housed in a big laundry between Erquinghem and Armentières.

We stayed in these billets for about a fortnight and spent Easter there. For Mass on Sundays I used the village churches at Erquinghem and Bac St Maur, but on weekdays I used a little oratory fitted up in a house near my billet by the priest attached to the Ambulance at Fort Rompu. On Maundy Thursday in Holy Week I went over to hear Confessions and say Mass for the Transport men of three of my Battalions who were all together in some outlying farms at a place called Le Point Mortier, about five miles away. There were thirteen who came to Mass and Communion in the little room placed at my disposal by the people of one of the farms.

On Friday, 13th April, the Brigade went back into the line again, and I occupied my old billet in Rue Marle. For the next few months life was very regular. On Sundays I used to say Mass in the handsome new Church of Notre Dame de Lourdes at Rue Marle, and a second one at Erquinghem, after which I generally heard Confessions there for about an hour, and subsequently lunched with the Curé. At Erquinghem the church was, as a rule, well filled, and the volume of men's voices singing the hymns at Mass, something I shall long remember. Living now with Lancashire units, the proportion of Catholics was far higher than what I had been accustomed to, and one sad result of this was that I had far more funerals than before. The cemetery chiefly used was that at Erquinghem, and one funeral I remember in particular of a man in the Liverpool Scottish, as it took place by the aid of lanterns almost at midnight.

Of the Battalions two were always in the line, one at Rue Marle and one in huts known as La Rolanderie, from the name of an adjacent farm. The Brigade held a line stretching roughly from the Lille road facing Wez Macquart to a place called Le Bridoux in front of Bois Grenier and facing Radinghem. I used now to pay frequent visits to the trenches, or rather breastworks, for that was what they really were. In this spring weather with everything in bloom they formed, especially on the left sector, an extraordinarily pretty network of flowering lanes and alleys. Those who knew them must remember as I do such places as Lille Post with its purple lilacs. Ferme de Biez with the water-lilies in its over-grown moat; Unley Road and Paradise Street and the Orchard. These of course were support lines; the actual front line hammered so often by " minnies " and shells was a very barren and desolate and unpleasant sort of place, with broken cemeteries and isolated graves, relics of the old days of 1914 when the line was first established here.

There were three main routes to get into the line. The first took one up the Lille road as far as Chapelle d'Armentières, where, at the cross-roads by the ruined church, one took to a trench leading off to the right The second was by way of a lane,

which branched off the Lille road where the railway
cuts it and led down to Ferme Desplanque and the
Battalion Headquarters for the left sector. The third
and prettiest was down by Rue Marle Church to
L'Armée, and thence through La Vesée to Ration
Farm and the Battalion Headquarters for the right
sector. I remember once, having gone up this way
and got right into the front line at a place called
Le Bridoux salient, watching an enemy aeroplane
crash, after having been engaged by one of ours. It
came tearing down, as I thought, right on top of us—
I was walking with another officer—and for a
moment I thought its purpose was to fire into the
trenches, when suddenly it burst into flames and fell
just over the parapet in "No Man's Land" The
pilot, as we afterwards found, was burnt to death.

Just as I visited the infantry in the trenches, so
also during all this period I had excellent opportunities of visiting the gunners, in their various
battery positions. These were generally located in
places where they might get some shelter from
observation, such as in ruined houses or clumps of
trees or orchards, and here the gunners were usually
very comfortable till the enemy took it into his head
to try and evict them, when things could be most
unpleasant. I managed once to get permission to
go up into an observation post used by the Field
Survey Company in conjunction with the heavy
gunners. The view from the top, aided by powerful
telescopes, was wonderful, and in the far distance over
the ridge—whence the enemy had unrivalled observation himself—one could just see the spires of Lille,
like signs of some Promised Land, in the far distance.

Once also I climbed up the inside of a tall factory chimney, used also for observation, but the thing kept swaying in such an alarming manner that I was glad to get down.

I had seldom occasion to go into Armentières. Sometimes on Sunday mornings I used to go to the Convent Chapel there to help in hearing Confessions whilst the chaplain was saying the nine o'clock Mass, and there was also a shop which nearly everyone visited from time to time. It was a depot for Burberry's, and was kept by one of the most enterprising shopwomen I have ever met. She had all her goods displayed to the best advantage, and the prices, though high, were not so terribly exorbitant as to deter customers. She had certainly done well for herself, for when I first saw her in May 1915 she had a very modest little shop indeed. Two or three evenings also I accepted an invitation to supper with M. l'Abbe D——, a charming French priest, in charge of the church of St Vast. He was living in his father's house, and had a most comfortable sitting-room with real English armchairs.

Armentières also boasted a restaurant, the "Au Boeuf," a very pleasant and popular resort with officers, and where we used to dine occasionally.

For seven weeks we enjoyed at Rue Marle an uninterrupted immunity from shells. One calm summer evening, 7th June, it received its first hammering. I was in the church giving Holy Communion when the first crash came, shivering the windows to pieces and covering the whole church with fragments. I hurried out, and almost the first thing I saw was one of our men lying dead in the street. The shells

were not, happily, coming over in bursts, but one by
one every few minutes. We had thirteen casualties,
some of them fatal, and the Gunners, Engineers, and
Machine Gunners all had casualties as well.

When everything had finally quietened down and the
wounded had been evacuated, we had dinner as usual
at Crown Prince House, and I was just preparing to
return to my billet when the shelling recommenced.
Hating to be alone, I decided to spend the night
with the others. In the middle of the night we were
roused from sleep and, so close were the shells
bursting, driven into the cellar. Here we found the
old couple who acted as caretakers, and we sat round
their fire nearly an hour, sipping coffee. Ultimately,
we retired again to bed. We were awakened early in
the morning by the heavy shelling of one of our
battery positions in a field a few hundred yards
away. We could see the whole thing from our
windows. In a few minutes the farm buildings just
behind the guns were set alight and huge columns
of smoke and flames shot out into the air. The
shelling continued more violent than ever, but
through the gallantry of the Major Commanding and
his men all the guns, but one, and large quantities of
ammunition were saved.

Henceforth, all sense of security around Rue Marle
was permanently destroyed. We had seen how
completely the enemy had the range of roads and
houses. Any moment he might, and frequently did,
recommence. His sudden activity was, I fancy, a
sort of counterblast to the recent capture of Messines
Ridge by us; and from this time forward his retaliation took the shape also of a constant shelling of

Armentières, with both high explosive and gas shells.
Casualties among the civilian population were very
high Day and night shells seemed to be constantly
skimming over our heads and dropping in clouds of
dust with a terrific explosion into the unfortunate
city. The afternoon seemed to be the quietest time,
and it was then that I went in once or twice with
our Adjutant to bathe in the Armentières swimming-
bath. Some enterprising engineers had got this going,
as far as water was concerned, and provided one kept
to the deep end, where there was no risk of treading
on broken glass, one could get an excellent swim.
In fact at one time it must have been a really first-
rate swimming-bath. The second time we went,
however, I noticed that the already damaged building
had altered so considerably for the worse, even during
the last few days, that I decided the pleasure was
not worth the risk of having to rush from its precincts
into some neighbouring cellar for safety, carrying
the few clothes one could grab in a hurry.

As the shelling of Rue Marle became now an
almost nightly occurrence, driving me out of bed
scantily clad, and hurrying me into a neighbouring
dug-out where our Pioneers lived, I decided to move
permanently to Crown Prince House, where I had
discovered a hitherto unoccupied room The house
stood alone between Rue Marle on the one side and
Chapelle d'Armentières on the other. It was still
practically intact, a square, modern, red brick house
with several fine rooms. The mess in particular was
a very pleasant room, with its big French windows
looking out on to a broad verandah, and over the
garden beyond. If necessary, the size of the room

could be almost doubled by opening the folding
doors which separated it from the next room. Thus
enlarged, we used it occasionally for Mess dinners,
at which all the Battalion officers were present. The
practical immunity from shell-fire which the house
so long enjoyed had—as commonly happens in such
cases—led to the current fiction of its belonging to
the Crown Prince, or at any rate of its destruction
being, by his orders, forbidden. The garden, though
largely overgrown and cut up by trenches, must at
one time have been quite a good one, and what
struck one most of all was the wonderful taste with
which the trees and shrubs had been chosen. When
these all burst into leaf at the first bloom of spring,
the blending tints of green and copper produced a
really beautiful effect. It used to be most pleasant
on cool summer evenings to wander round after
dinner. At one time, two or three evenings in
succession, we were entertained by aerial attacks on
our Observation Balloons. An enemy plane would
suddenly appear as if by magic out of a cloudless
sky and swoop down towards its prey, firing tracer
bullets furiously. The occupants of the balloon
would immediately fade away in their parachutes,
and amidst clouds of bursting anti-aircraft shells,
the balloon would very often come down in flames,
and the aeroplane withdraw untouched. ' One evening we saw as many as three brought down in
succession by the one plane.

It was on the last day of June that I moved into
Crown Prince House, and I stayed there till the
17th of July. My window looked ·north into
Armentières, and often I would look out towards

the city which, under the constant rain of heavy shells, was literally crumbling to ruin before my eyes. For some time now I had ceased to use Rue Marle Church. After the first shelling, I had always felt anxious when there were any large numbers present, and after cleaning it out one Saturday evening preparatory to Sunday, and finding it next morning covered again with brick dust and fragments of stone and shell, I gave it up definitely. Instead, I used a barn which the French priest who served the district had fitted up as a chapel, and where he transferred the necessary ornaments and vestments.

A most excellent thing introduced into our Battalion at this time by Colonel O—— was the habit of giving all the men, when out of the trenches, a day's complete holiday. They used to be marched down in the morning to a pleasant field on the banks of the Lys. Several would profit by the occasion to bathe in the river. After that they would sit about in the warm sunshine till dinners were served out from the "cookers" which we brought with us. Then the majority would lie out and sleep, making up now for our usually disturbed nights at Rue Marle, and some would take a walk till tea-time. After tea, everything would be packed up and the Battalion would march back to billets in the cool of the evening. It was a change which I think the men really enjoyed.

On Tuesday, 17th July, we left Crown Prince House and went into the trenches on the right sector of the Brigade front. I went into the line with the Battalion and lived in a cosy little shelter in what was known as the Subsidiary or Third Line and messed sometimes with Battalion Headquarters, sometimes with one of the companies if the former happened to be overcrowded. There was no chance now of daily Mass, but I used to bicycle every evening into Erquinghem for Confessions, and always kept up my Sunday Mass there.

Like Rue Marle, Erquinghem had for years been free from shelling till one evening its turn came too I was in the church when the first burst came over, and though no shells actually hit the building they came near enough to drive me and several others to take shelter in some neighbouring trenches. Happily the shelling did not last long, but it was enough even if there had been no casualties—as a matter of fact there were several—to destroy one's feeling of security here also. A few days later Rue Marle was heavily shelled again. This time Crown Prince House was absolutely destroyed and its beautiful garden turned into a fast withering wilderness. The next time I saw it no living thing was visible except a cat crawling about among the ruins. *Faute de mieux*, Erquinghem became the rest billets for the Battalion, which would otherwise have been at Rue Marle.

About every eight days we used to move back from the line and the Battalion round La Rolanderie would relieve us. On these occasions Battalion Headquarters would be at a farm known as "Artillery Farm," redolent now in my mind of fresh butter and smiling children and some really good horses and cows. I used, as a rule, to occupy, with two or three other officers, a room in the neighbouring Canteen Farm.

Our first incoming here was marked by an unfortunate incident. A Signaller, who had come out with the advance party from the trenches, was walking about the loft, where the men's beds were, when in the darkness he fell through a hole in the floor on to the cobbles of the stable beneath. When I saw him he was unconscious, and he died a few hours later in the hospital at Estaires where he was taken in an ambulance.

Another unfortunate thing happened during one of our stays at " Artillery Farm." I was riding one wet day into Estaires to see the chaplain there, when my horse slipped on the pavé and fell, cutting its knee badly and bringing me heavily on to my face. The accident, however, could hardly have happened at a more opportune place, for when I picked myself up and the agitated crowd had faded away, it appeared that on one side of the road were some horse-lines, where my animal was patched up, and on the other a Field Ambulance where I was attended to myself, and, moreover, kindly provided with a car to take me first into Estaires and then home to " Artillery Farm." The first doctor who saw me said there was no need to give me an anti-tetanus injection as I was merely suffering from abrasions of the skin. When a doctor at the Casualty Clearing Station at Estaires—where the chaplain lived—happened to see me, however, he wanted to force me to be inoculated, and on my still refusing, cheerfully declared it to be sheer suicide on my part. Happily his predictions remained unfulfilled, and in a few days all traces of my misadventure had disappeared.

P

On 3rd August we went back a second time to the Right Sector trenches, walking up, I remember, the whole way from "Artillery Farm" to the Battalion Headquarters in the line in our gas masks for practice. As in the Left Sector, so here also there were many pretty spots, including a quaint old farm—"Moat Farm"—near Crombalot Dump by Bois Grenier, and some pretty grass-grown flowering trenches round about the road running up to Le Bridoux.

It was also on the whole a moderately quiet sector, though by several raids, including one daylight one by the Liverpool Scottish, we used to stir up a certain amount of general unpleasantness, which would often bring reprisals on our own heads in the shape of raids, "minnies," and gas shells.

The alternation between the line and La Rolanderie billets went on till the middle of September. I used to keep up regularly my Sunday Mass at Erquinghem, and also, at this time, arranged an earlier Mass on Sundays at Fleurbaix for the benefit chiefly of the gunners in the neighbourhood. I shall always look back with pleasure to my visits here. A very pretty chapel had been fixed up by the Curé in an ordinary small house — the church, needless to say, being completely in ruins—and here Sunday by Sunday I said Mass for my little congregation. The gunners would come clanking in in their spurs, great strapping fellows for the most part, and like all our artillery, very smartly turned out, and mingle with the other soldiers and the few civilians who also came. Then after Mass and usually a few Confessions I used to ride off to Erquinghem for my second Mass, and finally lunch with the Curé.

It was also during these last days of August and the first days of September that we used to watch from "Artillery Farm" the last agony of Armentières. The shelling of the city and its suburbs was as continuous as ever, and large fires were constantly breaking out and blazing up unchecked. Of an evening the dull red glow of the burning city would light up the whole sky, and must have been visible for miles around. On one occasion I had to go to the big cemetery, "St Jean," on the western outskirts of Armentières to bury a gunner. It was a day of pouring rain, and as I waited for the arrival of the body, I noticed that the grave, where it was to be laid, was almost an inch deep in a nauseating mixture of water and blood, which was oozing out from the next grave. The stench was horrible, but there was nothing for it but to lay the body in, say the few brief prayers of the burial service, and then fill in the grave as quickly as might be.

On Monday, 17th September, we were relieved from "Artillery Farm" by a Battalion of the 38th Division and marched away to Estaires. The whole Division was being taken out for a month's rest. We stayed two days at Estaires, enjoying a very pleasant holiday, and meeting in the evenings for dinner at one of the hotels. It was here that Colonel O——, who had been wounded a few weeks back, rejoined us. On Wednesday, the 19th, we marched to Busnettes, stopping for dinner on the banks of the La Bassee Canal, just below Hinges. The next day we marched through Lillers to the little village of Laires, which was to be our final destination.

Apart from a Field Ambulance we had the village to ourselves, and soon made ourselves extremely comfortable. I shared a good billet with the Adjutant, and when the evenings began to get chilly and dark, the Doctor would join us, and we three would sit round the fire discussing life in general and the Battalion in particular. Our mess was in the Curé's house. The Curé was most pleasant, offering me the use of his church at any time, taking a great interest in the Battalion, and proving of real service to us in his quality as Mayor, by smoothing over those many little difficulties with the civilian population which inevitably arise where troops are billeted. He came and dined with us one night, and on another occasion, when some meeting of the local clergy was taking place, he invited me to the eminently clerical dinner which followed.

Each of the other three Battalions had their own village. The 2/4 South Lancs. were at Livossart, the 2/9 Liverpools at Febvin-Palfart, and the Liverpool Scottish at Flechin, and it was as usual my pleasant task to ride round during the week and visit them and arrange services for them.

Whilst we were at Laires we gave a dinner to the men of the Battalion. Large quantities of pork, beer, vegetables, and fruit were bought, and a lot of crockery hired. Since sufficient indoor accommodation could not be found, a field was chosen for the dinner, and on the appointed day everything was laid out on the ground on mackintosh sheets and the meal began. The weather, however, was the uncertain element in the proceedings, and unfortunately barely had every one set to on his plateful of pork, potatoes, and greens, when the rain started. Commencing with a few drops, it soon developed into a regular downpour, and I remember the Curé standing watching the sight under his dripping umbrella. The dinner, however, still went on, those who had not surrendered them for tables putting on their ground-sheets; but the rain destroyed the general pleasantness of things and very much shortened the festival. I know, however, that the men appreciated what the officers had endeavoured to arrange for them, and knew it was no fault of theirs that it was not the success it might have been.

The Mess-dinners for the officers went off better. We had two or three, and, as Mess President, a considerable amount of work devolved on me in the shape of hiring a room and crockery, and getting in the necessary supplies. We managed to get a room in one of the local estaminets, and with speeches and songs had some quite jovial evenings.

Brigade sports were another feature of our stay at Laires. They were held on some open ground just outside our village, and included besides the usual items and side-shows an officers' point to point, in which there were several entries, and which excited general interest.

Towards the end of our "rest" I instituted Night Prayers every evening at eight in the village church. Though there were never many there I think those who did come appreciated them as deeply as I did myself. We were on the eve of battle and knew it.

All through the last few weeks the Brigade had

been training vigorously, preparing to take part in the fighting round Ypres. The time of departure came at length, and on the morning of 18th October, having spent just four complete weeks there, we marched out from Laires.

CHAPTER VII

AROUND YPRES AND ARMENTIÈRES

It was a bright autumn morning when the 2/5 South Lancs. marched out from Laires some nine hundred strong, with drums beating and bugles playing. After a long march, during which we passed Aire on our right, we halted near Renescure, a few miles east of St Omer. The following morning, 19th October, the Battalion moved in buses to Proven, north-west of Poperinghe. The Transport, however, starting early, moved by road via Cassel, Steenvorde, and Watou, and I rode with them It was a long but interesting and picturesque journey. We left Renescure about five in the morning, and skirting the steep hill on which lies the town of Cassel, we halted for "dinners" just beyond Steenvorde. We reached Proven about six in the evening, and were directed to Privett Camp, a mile or so out of the town. We were surprised, on arriving, to find that the Battalion had not yet come in. It did not, in fact, reach camp till long after dark, and took almost as long stumbling over the muddy track which led out to the camp from Proven, as it had over the whole preceding distance.

We remained under canvas at Privett Camp for

five days.   The other Battalions were all in the
neighbourhood, and I used on Sunday the fine
spacious church at Proven which was central for
them all.   On Wednesday, 24th October, we moved
to Prattle Camp on the other side of Proven, and
here I was fortunate enough to find a chapel in a
Belgian hospital near by, which proved most useful
for Mass and Confessions.

One night there was a tremendous gale of wind
and rain.   The Mess marquee was blown down, and
frantic officers might have been seen that night
shivering in pyjamas, and striving to stave off ruin
from their own tents.

We left Prattle Camp about midnight on Friday,
marched into Proven, entrained, spent one or two
dismal hours in a cattle truck, and finally detrained
whilst it was yet dark at Elverdinghe, north of
Ypres.   After a period of chaotic confusion and
much waiting about on muddy roads, we at length
found quarters at Bridge Camp, and threw ourselves down on the bare floor of a Nissen hut for a
few hours' sleep.   I awoke about seven A.M. inde-
scribably cold and stiff, and with one or two officers
got up and walked amidst the ruins of the village,
principally to try and get warm, but also in hopes of
getting something warm to drink, for of breakfast
there seemed no earthly possibility in our own camp.
We ultimately got some canteen hands, we came
across, to give us some hot tea, which we drank with
much appreciation, seated on the ruins of the village
church

I remained at Bridge Camp till Monday, the 29th,
when I went up with my batman to the "Canal

Bank" where, after considerable difficulty, I at
length found a home with our Brigade Pioneers and
a mess with our Divisional Burials Officer. The
locality known as the "Canal Bank" consisted of a
long series of dug-outs and shelters, of varying
degrees of discomfort, built into the western bank of
the Ypres Canal. Advanced Divisional Headquarters
and several other units were all accommodated here,
as well as an Advanced Dressing Station.

On the 30th, the whole Brigade moved forward
towards the line. The attack, however, in which it
was to have taken part, was already cancelled. I
visited my own Battalion at Huddleston Camp and
the 2/4 South Lancs. at Marsouin Camp that day,
whilst they were waiting till it became sufficiently
dark for them to move farther forward.

Whilst I was living on the "Canal Bank" I paid
two visits to Langemarck—the farthest forward I
ever got on this front—to see our Divisional gunners
who were in action there. The first time I walked up
with one of the R.F.A. Medical Officers. It proved
a long, painful, and dangerous walk, over country
very similar to what I had already encountered on
the Somme. It was, however, more water-logged,
and for that very reason I think less muddy, as all
the water seemed to drain off into the shell-holes,
which were invariably filled almost to the brink, and
the remaining country was more or less solid and
dry; whereas on the Somme the whole face of the
earth was one heaving mass of thick, clinging mud
After several times losing our way we did eventually
reach Langemarck, only distinguishable from the
surrounding desolation by several prominent concrete

Q

"pill-boxes" and a broken fragment of the church.
The first "pill-box" we entered, where several
gunner officers were lying huddled together in the
dim light of a few candles, brought home to me in
most striking fashion the appalling nature of modern
war. Death, wounds, and destruction one is prepared to meet, but not a group of once healthy men
with eyes now bloodshot and running, and voices so
weak and husky as to be almost inaudible. Gas
alone had reduced them to such a state, and yet, in
spite of it all, they were extraordinarily cheery.

After paying a hurried visit to the other battery
positions around Langemarck, I made my way back
alone along the ill-omened road which ran past "Iron
Cross Corner" and over the Pilckem Ridge. The
second time I paid a visit to these regions I used, not
the road, but the duck-board tracks which stretched
—miles and miles of them—right up to the front line.

One day I accompanied the Divisional Burial
party in one of their early morning efforts. The
work was to search the forward areas in those hours
when things were supposed to be at their quietest,
collect the dead, and with or without a chaplain,
bury them in established cemeteries. On this particular morning, having, after no little difficulty,
contrived to collect our party we set forth gallantly
enough, but our own guns opening up a most
terrific barrage, it was thought, by the officer in
charge of the party, more expedient to withdraw
than to advance, and withdraw we consequently did,
with nothing accomplished.

On the whole, life on the Canal Bank was not
interesting, and I was very glad when on 6th

November I was able to return to Rear Battalion
Headquarters at Bridge Camp   On the previous day
the Battalion had been withdrawn from the front line
into support at "Eagle French," and two days later
it was taken out all together; and on Thursday,
8th November, the party at Bridge Camp rejoined
it by Boesinghe railway station.

That evening after waiting at the so-called station
—it was barren of any building—from 2 30 in
the afternoon till six in the evening, our train did
finally arrive, and we started off on a long journey
towards Calais   About midnight we arrived at
Audruicq where we were to detrain.   A fine, drizzling rain was falling, and the station yard was almost
ankle-deep in black, liquid mud.   We had to wait
nearly an hour whilst the men collected their blankets
and stacked them in bundles   At length the Battalion
formed up, and with our guide leading we marched
off.   The distance we had to cover was some fifteen
miles, a long march at the best of times.   In the
darkness the guide lost himself, and we had to pore
over maps with torches and guttering candles in
order to get back to the right road.   The men were
so tired after their spell in the line and the long
hours of waiting and travelling, that they fell out in
large numbers.   Still we pushed on, and dawn, a
beautiful rosy morning, found us mounting the last
hill which was to bring us in sight of our destination,
the village of Landrethun.   When we arrived we
found Battalion Headquarters to be in a real furnished
Château, such as a Divisional Headquarter Staff would
hardly have scorned, and seldom I think was hot
French coffee and fresh bread and butter more

appreciated than it was by us that morning. In a few hours the Battalion was comfortably settled in good billets, and sleeping off the toil of the last few days. Our own Château was quite a fine old building, belonging to the St Just family, and surrounded by a beautiful park from which, on fine days, one had a good view of Calais. Its only occupants, when we were there, consisted of a brother of the owner and two servants, one of whom, a typical old French retainer, looked after the wing of the house which we occupied and provided us with wood for the fires and coffee and fruit.

On Sunday, 11th November, I rode down to Audruicq—via Divisional Headquarters at Zutkerque where I got my "warrant"—and entrained there for Calais en route for England on my third "leave."

I rejoined the Battalion on 27th November, and was fortunate enough to have a motor-cycle and side-car lent me by a gunner-major I had met in the train to take me up from Audruicq Station to Landrethun. We had still ten more days to spend in this delightful district. The other Battalions were at Nielles, Zutkerque, and Recques, all some distance away, and necessitating some long but very pleasant rides. On one bright frosty morning I walked with the Doctor to Licques. The road mounted gently along a wooded slope and then from the crest zig-zagged sharply down an almost perpendicular cliff into the valley below. The view from the top over rolling hills and little villages, each with their church spire, was quite fine.

At length in the dark early hours of Friday, 7th December, we marched away from Landrethun and

entrained about nine o'clock at Audruicq Station.
Our train went up as far north as the picturesque,
mediæval looking city of Bergues, and then we bent
back south again and finally detrained at Proven.
From here we marched to billets in scattered farmhouses near Herzeele.   Two of the other Battalions
were in Herzeele itself, and the 2/4 South Lancs.
were at Wylder.   We remained in this area ten
days.   On Sundays I used the fine big church at
Herzeele, and on one occasion I went over to
Wormhoudt to see some Australians who had come
a few days previously, all the way to the isolated
farm where our Battalion Headquarters were, looking
for a priest, and, finding me out, had left a note to
say where they were, and asking me to come over.

On Monday, 13th December, we entrained on the
narrow gauge railway at Herzeele which took us to
the main line at Proven.   Here we entrained again
and got out finally at Boesinghe at half-past twelve.
Our camp, Boesinghe Camp, was only five minutes'
walk away, and we were soon settling in as comfortable
as we could.   We spent Christmas here.   For Mass
I used a Church Army Hut placed at my disposal by
the Church of England chaplain   It was a most convenient place, being practically in our own camp, and
served both for Sunday and Christmas Day.   In the
evenings it was used for concerts, and one night the
Battalion got up a concert of its own.   It was a great
success, but as I look back upon it, infinitely sad, as
so many who sang and listened and laughed there
were spending the last few hours of their lives, which
they were so soon to give up on the bleak, snow-
covered tracks leading up to Passchendaele and
Houlthust Forest.

The other Battalions were nearer Elverdinghe, where a Y.M.C.A. marquee was used for Mass by one of the other priests in the Division. The weather, all during these days, was bitterly cold. The Adjutant and I lived together in a sort of half dug-out and shelter, none too warm, and our own mess was in a Nissen hut where the chimney—in spite of constant attention and variation at the hands of our fireplace expert—continued to smoke abominably till the day we moved, when it started to go well.

On the evening of 24th December we had our Christmas dinner. All the officers of the Battalion managed to squeeze into our Nissen hut, and everything went off excellently. That same night, however, an advance party had to go up the line, and on Christmas Day, after Mass in the morning for the Roman Catholics and Christmas midday dinners for all, the whole Battalion followed, and occupied a part of the line opposite Houlthust Forest.

Two other officers and myself took charge of what was known as Advanced Quartermaster's Stores. We spent Christmas night in a deserted hut in a camp whose preceding occupants had been driven out by shelling, supping principally off the contents of a parcel, which arrived most opportunely, for an officer we all knew, who was at the time detached from the unit.

Next morning we moved our quarters into a hut a few hundred yards away, still on the east side of the Canal, and just below Baboon Camp. Though cold and draughty in the extreme we had, however, four wire beds here, which was something ; and we fixed

up an apology for a mess in a neighbouring hut. I
have seldom been so cold or uncomfortable as during
these days: still I was very glad I had taken up
my quarters here as I was able to see the Catholics
in the 2/4 South Lancs. in Baboon Camp before
they went up to the line, and also say Mass for
and give a General Absolution and Communion to
several lads in my own Battalion who were to form
part of a raiding party which came back to Baboon
Camp for twenty-four hours' so-called rest. The object
of this raid was to regain a certain "Turenne Crossing
which a battalion in the line before us had lost.
Colonel O—— came down himself from the line and
spent a day with us, in order the more conveniently
to arrange the details, and be in touch with the
Brigade who were just a few minutes' walk in front
of us. At length, after several hours of feverish
activity and much writing of orders, everything was
ready, and one dark evening I saw Colonel O——
off in the mess-cart which was to take him, as far
as it could go, up the line

Hitherto the nights had all been bright and frosty
and the ground white with snow. The night of the
raid was black as pitch, and it was due to the darkness that the raiding party lost direction and failed
of their main objective. We lost during our stay in
the line and in the course of the raid several fine
young officers and men, killed and wounded and
missing. I was not sorry to leave this part of the
country, with its flat, muddy, broken roads and general
desolation. We entrained again at Boesinghe on
the afternoon of 2nd January, and detrained about
an hour later at Ondank, only a few miles away,

and took up our quarters at De Wippe Camp just off the Elverdinghe-Poperinge road, and about six or seven miles from the latter town.

The following day I had the opportunity of seeing M—— whom I had not met since we shared a tent together at Gezaincourt. He was now M.O. to an Army Brigade R.F.A., and was living a few miles from our camp. I lunched with him that day, and he walked back with me and had tea with us.

On Friday, the 4th, we marched to International Corner—over roads which I remember were so slippery that one could scarcely walk—and entrained about ten in the morning. We detrained at Bailleul, and marched from there along the old familiar road through Nieppe to Pont-de-Nieppe, where we were to be billeted.

This place was sadly changed from what I had known it in 1915. There were no civilians here now, most of the houses were damaged and some absolutely in ruins, and the church was badly knocked about and closed. We all, however, soon made ourselves quite comfortable, as several of the houses, though devoid of furniture, were still quite habitable, and the surrounding ruins furnished an unfailing source of fuel.

We stayed here till 13th January. For Mass I used a big cinema hall which, though very dark, served its purpose quite well both for Sundays and weekdays. The other three Battalions were in camps nearer Steenwerck, and for them the church there was fairly accessible.

On the afternoon of 13th January we went into the line in front of Houplines. Our way took us through Armentières, and we had an opportunity of seeing how great and widespread was the ruin caused by the long summer bombardments of the preceding year. The great Church of St Vaast was a mere shattered, empty crust, with nothing but ruins within, and almost every house, of those still standing, was badly damaged.

In the line the Doctor and I lived at the Regimental Aid Post at what was known as Tissage Dump, a big ruined factory standing just on the western outskirts of Houplines. Our cellar was really most comfortable. There was one large chamber fitted with several beds where we could keep the sick, and where our own personnel slept, a second large room used as the Dressing-Room and containing a good stove for boiling water and cooking, and finally, off this, our own room which was comfortably furnished with tables and chairs, a sofa, cupboard, and a good fireplace. We slept in two tiny rooms which gave on to a little passage leading out of our sitting-room The only drawback to the whole place was the danger of being flooded out: at one time the floor of the Dressing-Room was nearly an inch deep in water, but by pumping we managed as a rule to keep the place fairly dry. Being so cosy, our R.A P. was naturally a popular resort, and often the Headquarter officers, when off duty, or before going out on a night duty, would spend an hour or two with us. We could always raise some tea, and had several very cheery evenings.

If we at Battalion Headquarters or the Aid Post were comfortable enough, the men were extremely badly off. After a few hours' rain the trenches became

к

absolutely water-logged, there were very few dry
shelters, and the men in the front line posts could
only be got at by night.   Consequently hot meals were
impossible.   Nothing cooked, where it was possible to
cook at all, would ever reach the front line in other
than, at best, a tepid state, and as for changing into
dry socks, and feet rubbing, the whole idea, seeing the
conditions under which the men lived and worked,
was impossible.   Much sickness and trench-feet was
the inevitable result.   Every day I used to walk up the
line as far as it was possible to go without "waders."
All the Company Headquarters were get-at-able,
but however muddy and wet I got, I always had a
great but selfish feeling of relief in knowing I had a
dry, warm spot to retire into for the night.

On Friday, 18th January, the Battalion was withdrawn into the Subsidiary Line, and Battalion
Headquarters and the Headquarter Company were
billeted in houses by the level-crossing where the
railway line cuts the Armentières-Erquinghem road.
On Monday the whole Battalion returned to its old
billets in Pont-de-Nieppe.   Here we had the first
news of an important change about to take place,
and destined to affect us all personally very much.
It had been decided to reduce the strength of
brigades from four to three battalions, and in each
brigade one battalion was to be either detached or
disbanded and its personnel sent to reinforce other
units.   For reasons which in no way reflected on its
efficiency, the 2/5 had been chosen to be disbanded.
The day before the announcement was made
public the colonel took me aside into his room and
told me about it.   I was absolutely dumbfounded,

as no idea of any such thing happening had ever occurred to me. Next evening we had a final dinner at which all the officers of the Battalion were present. Several speeches were made and toasts drunk, but the news of the coming separation announced by the Colonel in a short speech hung over us like a shadow, and prevented the meeting from being the wholly pleasant one it would otherwise have been.

On Sunday, 27th January, the Battalion went into the line for the last time, but the Colonel and Adjutant went for one night to the billet we had occupied by the level-crossing to work out the details of the disbanding, and I accompanied them. Next morning, however, I went up to the line, and the other two followed in the evening. After two days, during which I lived as before with the Doctor at Tissage Dump, the Battalion came back to Armentières and was billeted in and around the big Convent there, with the chapel of which at anyrate I was already familiar, as I had said Mass there on three or four occasions lately. The rest of the building was bare, cold, and draughty in the extreme.

On 1st February the first party to go, one hundred men and two officers, went off to the 1/5 South Lancs. in the 55th Division. Next day the remainder of us moved to Menegate Camp, just outside Steenwerck. This was a very dreary time. The future for all of us was vague, and would probably entail once more that painful process of slowly building up new groups of friends and acquaintances. Every day almost brought its partings and final handshakes, and some further party of men and officers would leave us. Quite a number went to the 2/4

South Lancs., some went to the Base, some to Brigade, some to the Flying Corps, and the remainder were in the end attached temporarily to an Entrenching Battalion. When the Colonel left us for a month's leave in England I thought it time to look about for myself.   I knew, however, I should not have long to wait nor far to look for a good home, and among officers I knew well already.   My transfer to the 2/4 South Lancs. was soon arranged, and I joined them on Sunday, 10th February, at Waterlands Camp behind Erquinghem.

CHAPTER VIII

REST AND A HURRIED DEPARTURE

THE day after I arrived at Waterlands Camp, where I was most kindly welcomed by everyone, the 2/4 South Lancs moved to the Laundries between Erquinghem and Armentières with one Company pushed forward into the Subsidiary Line. We were only here, however, a few days, and on the 15th marched off to Estaires, the whole Division being withdrawn from the line for a month's rest. Estaires, of course, was the height of luxury. The men were all accommodated in a large warehouse overlooking the river Lys, and every officer I think had a room to himself. My own billet was over a grocer's shop, or rather a general provision store, kept by three sisters and their brother who had been invalided out of the French Army. They had thousands of francs' worth of goods always on their premises, and their shop was well known for miles around to all the officers' messes. Our own Mess-room was in a house by the church, and though the people of the house were only indifferently pleasant, we were really very comfortable there. There were six others in our Headquarter mess besides myself, all of whom I

knew before, and excellent company ; and Lieut.-Col
M—— who commanded the battalion, was one of the
most charming men it has ever been my pleasure
to meet.

We remained at Estaires for a full month. My
own life was uneventful in the extreme. Of the
other Battalions, one was in Estaires with us, and
one a mile or so away around Neuf Berquin. I used
habitually on Sundays and weekdays the fine
church at Estaires. For several days I kept in
touch with the relics of the 2/5 South Lancs., both
the Transport which was remaining complete at
Menegate Camp, and whom I visited for Easter Confessions and Communion, and also the others, men
and officers, who were with the Entrenching Battalion
at Doulieu. On two or three occasions also I rode
over to where the artillery were between Le Sart
and Haverskerque, and once got so far afield as
Bethune, where I went in a motor ambulance for a
chaplains' meeting. I also paid several visits to
Merville Whilst we were in Estaires we had, one
afternoon, a very excellent Brigade Horse Show, and
one of the Field Ambulances got up a first-rate
concert party which functioned every evening and
was well worth seeing. Not a little of my time also
I spent in visiting outlying units of the Machine
Gun Corps, and enabling them to get to their Easter
duties. On the whole, as is evident, my life was
extremely peaceful and quiet.

Towards the end, however, of our stay, Estaires
was subjected, for the first time since 1914, to hostile
shelling. I was just finishing Mass on the morning
of Wednesday, 13th March, when I heard an ominous

whizz and crash. On leaving the church a few minutes later the same sounds were repeated, and this time there could be no question as to what it was. For nearly two hours shells continued coming over at intervals of about ten minutes, dropping mostly by the bridge over the river at the eastern end of the town, or right over on the outskirts towards the north. Though casualties were happily few, the panic among the civilian population was extreme, and the road out towards Neuf Berquin was very soon black with women and children hurrying away and carrying what few household utensils they could lay their hands on as they fled. Several, I fancy, returned again that night, but the custom of going away in the evening and sleeping in farms or villages a few miles behind, and then coming back next morning, prevailed henceforth among many. The people in my own billet were constantly asking me how I viewed the situation, and whether I should advise them to retire with their goods to a house they had in Merville, a course I knew they would be very loath to take. I could but tell them, what was the general opinion, that the recent shelling was very probably a natural retaliation on the enemy's part for our own shelling of some of his back areas.

There was, however, undoubtedly a general suspicion that the enemy might also be preparing an offensive on a big scale on this front. All the units of our Division had their battle positions allotted to them in case an attack developed, a scheme of defensive trenches was laid out and the digging of them actively pressed forward, and one day Sir Douglas Haig came round to inspect them in person. They were known as the

Lys Defences, since that river was to form the main defensive line.

One night things came to such a pitch that we found ourselves on half an hour's notice to move, and had in consequence to sleep with our clothes on, and almost every morning now at dawn our guns put down a "protective barrage" on what were regarded as likely assembly positions for the enemy. Nothing, however, happened, and though the shelling of Estaires was twice repeated before we left, the scare of a German attack gradually faded away.

On the day before we left Estaires, I went up towards Fleurbaix to see if I could find a suitable place for Mass, since I thought the Battalion would be probably going into the line there. I met the Curé who served these parts, and learnt from him that the little chapel I had used before in Fleurbaix had been given up, but that there was now one just outside the village in a farm called Porte à Clous. This I went to see, and found the chapel fixed up in the stables of the farm, which was being used as a Brigade Headquarters. On my way home I was delayed by heavy shelling in the vicinity of the bridge which crossed the river between the villages of Bac St Maur and Croix de Bac. I was just passing a "traffic control post" when a shell dropped near the bridge on my right, hurling fragments all round. I turned back to wait awhile, when the man on duty shouted to me to go on. "Now's your time, sir," he said, "you've got five minutes before the next one comes," and so I started doubling down the deserted village street of Bac St Maur with my footsteps ringing on the cobbles. When I had passed the danger zone I slackened off and looked out for a car or lorry to give me a lift back to Estaires. A minute or so later I heard another crash behind me by the bridge and immediately afterwards the sound of a motor. I looked round but saw immediately there was no chance of a lift here. It was the Corps Commander's car coming down the street at top speed It went past me like a flash. Luckily I was soon overtaken by a motor ambulance which took me right back to our Mess without further incident.

The following day, 20th March, we moved out of Estaires, and the Battalion went into the line between Fleurbaix and Laventie. I went with the "details" to Magog Camp behind Sailly. Six days later the Battalion came out of the line—where I had paid them one visit—and moved into close support near Rouge de Bout, where I rejoined them. Battalion Headquarters were in two farmhouses on the road between Rouge de Bout and Fleurbaix, with two companies in farms in front and two behind.

Meanwhile news had come of the great German drive towards Paris, and all fears of an attack on our front were definitely dismissed. Rumours of a speedy move were rife, but for the moment Rouge de Bout, in spite of occasional shelling, proved a comfortable home. It was, however, too near the front line for Mass, but I managed to hear the Easter Confessions of several of the men—as I had done from Magog Camp of the other battalions in this area—and when Easter Sunday came I went to say Mass in the little temporary chapel at Croix de Bac. Large numbers were there, especially of the artillery, a staff officer served my Mass, and everything in the village on that sunny Easter morning seemed bright and cheerful. That same evening, however, 31st March, we were off, bound for the south, and as we confidently anticipated, for battle. We marched first to billets at Neuf Berquin.

Our place was taken by an enfeebled Division, weakened and reduced in numbers during the recent fighting in the south. Ten days later the enemy made his second great drive, this time towards Calais and the coast, involving in bitter destruction all the smiling villages and gay little French towns of this country we had got to know so well.

On the afternoon of Monday, 1st April, we moved to Le Parc, a little village pleasantly situated in a big clearing in the midst of the vast Forêt-de-Nieppe. The next night we marched in pouring rain to Steenbecque Station, where we entrained about midnight. After the usual unpleasant journey we detrained at Doullens at about half-past seven next morning, and marched to billets in Beaudricourt. The following evening we were off again, this time to Sombrin, which we reached about eleven that night, once more in the pouring rain. Here we were fortunate enough to be allowed to stay till Monday, and so we made ourselves comfortable. The Liverpool Scottish were with us in the same village, and the 9th Kings were at Warluzel, about two miles away. On Sunday I said a Mass here, as well as one at Sombrin. On Monday we moved.

We left Sombrin at half-past eight in the morning, and marching via Pas, Thievres, and Famechon, ultimately halted at an old aerodrome at Marieux, where we were housed in huts. The march was a most exasperating one, as we were continually passing through villages thought to be our destination, but which on arrival proved to be completely lacking in sufficient accommodation. Whilst the colonel went on ahead to try and fix up billets at Marieux, we halted by the roadside and shared the men's "dinners," eating thankfully Maconochie rations out of a Maconochie tin, and drinking that strong oversweetened tea which the men seem to like so much.

Whilst we were at Marieux we heard the news of the great German attack round Armentières, and the fall of that town. The enemy seemed to have hood-winked us completely, for no sooner had we withdrawn most of our troops from that area, and replaced them by weaker divisions, than he attacked precisely where we had long expected him to, but whence his big drive down south had completely diverted our attention.

We stayed at Marieux till Friday when we marched back again to the Sombrin area, though this time we occupied Warluzel, and the 9th Kings went to our old billets at Sombrin. On Saturday we moved again, leaving as usual in the evening, and eventually about half-past ten, after a most tiring march, ended up in a damp, rain-sodden wood just above Pas. We passed a most uncomfortable night in the rain, covered with a tent which had arrived so late that we decided to use it as a blanket instead of selecting a suitable spot in the darkness to pitch it. Huddled underneath the heavy folds we tried, as best we might, to pass away the hours till morning. Next day, Sunday, Mass was out of the question, but I got the Catholics together and had a short service concluding with a General Absolution, as we were all expecting to be hurried any moment into a battle. On Tuesday, after we had just finished making ourselves fairly comfortable where we were, and when the men had all built for themselves ingenious little shelters of sticks and mackintosh sheets, we had to move to another wood a mile or so away between Henu and St Amand. Here we had to start all over again, building up a more or less habitable camp. This we finally succeeded in doing, after the tardy arrival of tents and bivouac sheets.

Meanwhile, the news of the war continued to grow blacker and blacker. North and south the enemy continued his great forward thrusts. A further attack on our own front was regarded as most certainly imminent, and frantic efforts were being made to counteract it. Trenches now covered all those back areas which in 1915 I had known as peaceful, solitary spots far removed from the turmoil of war. Our own battle positions were allotted to us, and the building of dug-outs pressed vigorously forward. Practice schemes both of defence and counter-attack, involving long days of reconnaissance, were frequently carried out. Still the great attack hung fire, and the days slipped by and the woods began breaking into bloom, and May came and found us still in our camp at Henu. But towards the end of April the monotony was broken suddenly by the unexpected news that the 2/10 Liverpool Scottish was to be amalgamated with its first line battalion the 1/10 Liverpool Scottish, and that their place in our Brigade was to be taken by the 1st Royal Munster Fusiliers.

On Saturday afternoon, 27th April, the Munsters arrived at Henu; and the 2/10 Liverpool Scottish, with many good friends of mine amongst them, went away the same evening.

.

PART II

Six Months with the First Munsters

CHAPTER I

OLD SCENES REVISITED

ON 3rd May 1918 I was attached to the Royal
Munster Fusiliers, so I left our camp in the wood
and went into Henu village. Two days later,
Sunday the 5th, we moved into the line with
Battalion Headquarters in old German dug-outs on
the eastern fringe of Gommecourt village.

We left Henu about half-past six, moved up by
road to Souastre, and then struck across country
towards Gommecourt, passing by the Château de la
Haie and leaving Foncquevillers on our left.

Progress was very slow, and as we left the Château
darkness began to fall, and with it a thin, penetrating
rain. The scenes to me were all strangely familiar.
Foncquevillers, for so many months a peaceful home,
was now a place to be sedulously avoided A
Battalion marching up that same night and passing
through the village street did not emerge unscathed,
and, as we moved forward, we could hear the heavy
shells bursting round the ruined church a few hundred
yards away. Only once during our stay in this
area did I revisit that well-known street I was on
a bicycle at the time, and spent little time there;
but I managed to get a glimpse of my old room in

T

the Dressing Station, still standing, all but its window, as I had known it almost three years before. Another thing I noticed was the number of bright little red-tiled cottages, built by the French civilians after the German retirement in March 1917. Now, of course, they were no longer occupied. Many were already shattered by shrapnel, and their emptiness stood in silent protest against the premature notices set up in French and English declaring the surrounding ruins to be national monuments, and on no account to be touched or altered.

Leaving Foncquevillers behind us on our left, we made our way up into Gommecourt village by an old trench which opened out into the sunken road connecting the two villages. Shells began to fall alarmingly near us, and the darkness, as it invariably does, only seemed to bring them nearer. Long shall I remember waiting in the inky blackness in that sunken road, cowering against the bank as the shells came over, with a file of men stretching dimly away in front, limbers and wagons struggling to get by, voices shouting out for lost platoons, and over all the drizzling rain, the weird glare of occasional " Very " lights and the burst of shells After interminable delays the Doctor and I at length reached Battalion Headquarters about half-past ten. There a guide was waiting to take us up to the Regimental Aid Post, which was some twenty minutes' walk farther on through muddy trenches. We got in about eleven, and seldom did I appreciate more the hot cocoa we soon got ready.

That first relief, walking up as we did in rear of the whole Battalion, in pitch darkness and falling

rain and persistent shell-fire, seemed a bad opening
for the coming days, but in reality the worst was
over as far as we two were concerned. The trenches,
it is true, under constant rain, came to be almost
impassable, but our casualties were slight. The
Doctor and I slept in the Aid Post and messed at an
adjoining Company Headquarters. Unlike the Aid
Post the dug-out here had only one entrance; besides
the officers, it was crowded with men, and some
Machine Gunners also occupied one end of it, so that
it was not surprising that the atmosphere inside
was appallingly thick. Several of us used to play
poker in the evenings, but I, personally, could never
endure to sit there for long and used to get out on
top for fresh air.

On the 9th of May we were relieved and moved
back into Gommecourt village, where almost all the
men were accommodated in deep dug-outs. Battalion
Headquarters was in a dug-out in the old German
front line, on the fringe of Gommecourt Park, which
for so many months had loomed up menacingly
against our old front line between Hebuterne and
Foncquevillers. The Regimental Aid Post was in a
roomy but far from shell-proof cellar or crypt under
what once had been the village church.

Our first night in Gommecourt Park, like our first
"relief" night, was bad. Several casualties occurred
in the village just after the Doctor and I had passed
through, and he was called back to give assistance,
whilst I went on to get stretcher-bearers. All the
wounded were finally got in, dressed, and evacuated.

Whilst we were here the weather mended and the
heat became quite intense, as intense, to my mind,

during the last weeks in May and the month of June, as it ever is in France. Gommecourt Park during these hot spring days was a wonderful place. The ground was all covered with thick undergrowth and full of wild flowers. The trees, torn by shells and blighted by gas, bearing all the scars of the great Somme battle, still lived in innumerable small shoots which spread out round the base of the trunk, rich and green.

Our Aid Post was a double one, *i.e.*, we shared it with the Doctor of the Battalion, holding the right of the Brigade sector, which happened, whilst we were there, to be the 2/4 South Lancs. It was, in consequence, a place of some importance, and the Engineers were, all the while, hard at work turning it into a really safe place, though it was still far from finished when we left.

On the night of Tuesday, 21st May, the Battalion moved back to reserve, leaving two companies in rear of Gommecourt, in what had facetiously been named "Beer Trench" Battalion Headquarters, and one Company went to the Château de la Haie, and one Company farther back still, to that wonderful old farm overlooking Coigneux village, "Rossignol Farm." The Château de la Haie, which in 1915 had housed a Brigade Headquarters, was now nothing but a literally hollow pretence, showing still a fine front, if one withdrew a few hundred yards away, but within largely lacking both floors and ceilings. We managed, however, to patch up a small room to serve as a Mess, and we all slept in a good safe cellar beneath. Only once did we have to take refuge here by day, and that was in the afternoon of

the day on which we went back to the line, when
much of our interest in the fate of the house had
lapsed. In spite of the shelling, however, we left it
much as we had found it, though I believe subsequently it was burnt to the ground.

Our stay at the Château lasted eight days. The
old loft, where I used to say my weekly Mass, was
unapproachable now, as the steps had been completely broken away, but I used instead the stables
beneath, which served just as well. The stabling was,
in fact, the chief feature of the whole building, and
must at one time have been extremely fine; in fact
the whole property was reputed to have originally
belonged to a "trainer." The garden was, of course,
wild and overgrown, but in those hot May days it
afforded, with its fine trees and shrubs, a shady
refuge from the hot dusty roads outside, which
was most welcome. We left it on Wednesday,
29th May.

This time we were to occupy the Left Sector of the
Divisional front, with "Pigeon Wood" behind us and
the "Bois de Biez" on our left. The Adjutant,
Doctor, and I walked up together. It was a lovely
evening and our walk was as peaceful as we could
wish till we got to the eastern outskirts of Gommecourt Here we heard a few shells dropping along the
open track, some half a mile in length, which led
straight out from the village into the trench where
Battalion Headquarters was. We left the cover of
the trees, hoping the "hate" was finished, and had just
started along the track when a regular shower of
light shells came dropping all around us. The other
two on my right dropped instantly into a convenient

shell-hole. I made for another just in front, only to find it full of slimy green water, so I cowered flat to the ground where I was ; then in a momentary lull we all ran forward to the shelter of a little bank in front. As I ran, impeded with a heavy haversack, water-bottle, tin hat, box respirator and other impedimenta, I felt that weird nightmare sensation of trying hard to run and yet being unable to make any progress ; the little sheltering bank seemed to recede farther and farther away. We did reach it at length in safety, and after a short breathing space, proceeded at a brisk walk towards the line, keeping well away from the clearly defined track in case the Hun thought of harassing it again. Battalion Head-quarters was reached at last, and, once the outgoing unit had gone, we all settled down for our trip in the trenches very much as one settles the rugs and papers and luncheon-baskets and bags preparatory to a long and rather boring railway journey.

In this part of the line the Aid Post was next to Battalion Headquarters, so the Doctor and I slept and messed there with the others. One night I was startled out of my sleep by heavy shelling and the sound of the Colonel's voice shouting to his servant for his revolver. I had visions of the enemy coming down into the dug-out. Happily they never got so far. A raid, however, was obviously in progress and we all "stood to," including our venerable Orderly-Room Corporal, who after carefully packing up all his papers in case it should prove necessary to beat a hurried retreat, leisurely ascended the dug-out steps, and, after looking out over the parapet with his rifle to his shoulder, remarked to his neighbour, "There seems little enough doing after all." Things were, in fact, gradually quietening down, no casualties came in, and it finally transpired that the raid had been not on our own front but on the right. As dawn broke I started to walk round the support Company's lines with the Colonel. At one point the trench was very low, and looking over I had a fine view of one or two German wagons hurrying away across a track behind their lines, similar to that behind ours, and being harassed as they went by our own fire. Besides this spot there was another better and safer observation post in this sector, which I used often to visit. From it one could see the smoke of the trains in Achiet-le-Grand Station, and far away to the south, the dim outline of Loupart Wood, with the chimneys of Bapaume beyond. Right in front lay the ruins of Serre, and I used often to see Germans in ones and twos going in and out.

One evening the artillery made an effort to set fire to Rossignol Wood This wood lay right in front of us in a re-entrant angle of our line, and was a source of constant danger, annoyance, and suspicion as we knew the enemy occupied and was working in it. The proceedings were timed to take place after dark, our front line posts were withdrawn—a wise precaution, in case any of our shells should fall short—and the show opened as planned. It proved a wonderful display. The whole wood was lit up for nearly an hour by a constant stream of thermite and inflammatory shells; then the curtain fell, and, next morning, there was the wood to all appearances the same as the day before Our endeavour to set the green wood alight had certainly failed. It was not till some weeks later that it was captured by the New Zealanders.

Our Mess though small was cosy enough and moderately comfortable, and we all slept in various holes and corners leading off it. Underneath the Doctor and I, slept three if not four runners heaped together. One of them, C——, was a famous character in the Battalion. He was a great talker, and if ever a letter arrived for him with the evening mail, he would discuss its contents with his bed-fellows till far into the night, smoking all the while cheap cigarettes, of which the fumes would ascend to our bunk above. He was also a heavy sleeper and much appreciated his quarters in the dug-out, as apparently my presence in the bunk above deterred the Sergeant-Major from using the only language which could rouse C—— from his slumbers.

Much of our time was spent wandering round the trenches and sitting with the others at the entrance to our dug-out, and in the evenings I used often to play chess with some of the Company officers. One morning I went over to the Company who were in reserve and who lived in a shallow trench half way between Battalion Headquarters and Gommecourt. I joined them at lunch, which they had in the open; but this particular morning the enemy started ranging over us with high-bursting shrapnel, and the fragments showed such continued and persever-ing efforts to mingle with the food that we were finally compelled to take refuge in a tiny dug-out meant for one, but destined, on such occasions as this, to accommodate four or five. Here we were imprisoned with shells bursting all round us for nearly an hour.

We left this sector on Friday, 14th June, and went right out to a camp in Couin Wood. This once had been a pretty spot, indeed I had known it as such before, but its continued use as a camp had fouled the ground, and heavy rains made it extremely damp. An order had come out that all tents were to be sunk three feet as a protection against bombing; but when the Doctor and I endeavoured to comply with it we came upon such quantities of unsavoury matter that we hastily moved our tent elsewhere, and ceased to disturb the soil again. Before we left Couin, the Division put up a mule race. We had in our Transport an extremely fast animal, and the "Munster Mule" became famous from that day, winning the race easily and incidentally filling several pockets and emptying others.

We left Couin for our final trip in the line on Sunday, 23rd June. We went back to the same sector we had occupied originally, and the Doctor and I, as before, lived at the Regimental Aid Post and messed with the neighbouring Company. We found the whole line much improved. The Regimental Aid Post had been enlarged, the Company Headquarters' dug-out had been also extended and a second entrance put in, which improved the atmosphere beyond measure, and above all, the whole system of trenches was dry and duck-boarded, so that, where before it had taken half an hour to get up to the front Company Headquarters, now the same round could be done in five or six minutes. There was one part of the line I shall always remember.

U

It was on our right, where the trench from being very deep suddenly crossed over a road—the one, I think, from Hebuterne to Serre—giving one a good view of the country forward. That particular spot used to exercise a sort of fascination over me, and I often went there. The Saturday before we were relieved I walked out of the line and spent the night at our Transport Lines near Coigneux. Next morning I said Mass at Rossignol Farm and after breakfast walked back to Gommecourt. As I was making my way along the trench from Battalion Headquarters to the Aid Post, whom should I meet but the Corps Commander and a glittering staff. He asked me what sort of sermon I had preached that morning, and promised to send me some notes.

The following day, Monday, 1st July, we were relieved by a New Zealand Division, and that night I walked back with the Doctor and Signalling Officer to Souastre. Here buses were waiting which took the whole Battalion to Louvencourt. We got in about four in the morning, and the same afternoon moved to a camp in a wood overlooking the village of Authie from the south.

Here we remained for a month. There was usually training in the morning, games and amusements in the afternoon and evening. The 9th Kings had their camp next to ours, and the South Lancs. and Brigade Headquarters were at St Leger, a mile or two away. I went on leave from Authie and so missed most of what went on, but I know, in the sports which were held at this time, the Munsters carried away both the Brigade and Divisional cups.

One sad incident occurred before I left. Two men

weie boiling a mess-tin of tea over an improvised
fire when there was a sudden explosion. A man
passing by at the time was killed instantly, one of
those making tea was so badly injured that he died
later in hospital, and the other, though not so
seriously wounded, was still badly hurt. Apparently
they had built their fire over one of those partially
buried bombs, of which hundreds must still be litter-
ing the war zone of France. The next afternoon I
buried the unfortunate victim in Couin Cemetery, and
the following morning left for England.

CHAPTER II

On Friday, 26th July, I rejoined the Battalion at Authie, and the following Monday we marched north. Our first halting-place was Saulty, where we stopped for the night. The next day we moved up to a camp on the main Arras-St Pol road near the village of Etrun. Our Mess President distinguished himself during those two marches by miraculously producing champagne for lunch at our midday halts. On Wednesday we moved into Arras and had most comfortable billets for the night. On Thursday evening we went into the line.

The Battalion held a line astride the Gavrelle road about half a mile west of that village and some six or seven miles east of Arras. Battalion Headquarters was in a dug-out cut into the side of a deep railway cutting on the old main line from Arras northwards to Lens. It was not without difficulty that we finally established ourselves here, as our original Headquarters was to have been in a sort of home-made house, lying under the shelter of the western slope of the ridge through which ran the cutting. On arriving there that evening we learnt from the outgoing unit that the other Headquarters

144

were going to be evacuated that night and left empty, and so the Colonel decided to take them over at once before anyone else got hold of them. Accordingly, as soon as the battalion relief was complete, and we had had dinner, we packed up our belongings and moved off. Striking the railway line just in front of us, we turned to the right and followed it, till we reached the cutting where the new Headquarters were. Going was not too easy. The whole track had been at one time heavily shelled and was in places piled up with white chalk boulders, which led some Lancashire lads we met, to make rude but facetious remarks on Alpine climbing. We ultimately found our quarters all right, though, just as we arrived, O'R—— discovered he had left his gas mask behind at the last place and had to hurry all the way back for it.

Our line ran roughly north and south along a ridge which was a sort of continuation of the famous Vimy Ridge. The reserve line was on the western slope, and from it one had a magnificent view behind of the ruined city of Arras, with its gaunt, shattered Cathedral rising up prominently in the midst. The support lines were on the summit and eastern slope, and commanded a fine view of the great Lens plain Henin Lietard was just visible on the extreme north, and straight in front the spires and towers of Douai stood out clearly in the distance, and at one's feet lay the ruins of Gavrelle.

River bathing was also a feature of this part of the line. Quite a good bathing-place, complete with spring-board, had been fixed up on the banks of the Scarpe, which, not far from our Battalion Head-

quarters, passed under the railway at a point where
a high embankment afforded complete shelter from
all enemy activity except anti-aircraft shells, which
occasionally, falling either entire or in fragments,
were liable to disturb the bathers.

We had no casualties this trip, till the very last
morning, 9th August, when for the first time the
enemy shelled what we had come to regard as our
inviolable cutting. The first shell dropped just outside my little concrete shelter as I was shaving, and
so badly wounded a man who was standing there
that he died soon afterwards. That morning I did
not say Mass, but till then, every morning, including
one Sunday, I had been able to say Mass in the
morning and Rosary in the evening in an old disused
Nissen hut which stood in the middle of the cutting.

On being relieved we went back to Aubrey
Camp on the Arras-Lens road, about a mile from
the ruined village of Roclincourt. Whilst we were
here I paid a visit to the Poor Clare Nuns who were
in Arras. I found their convent — their *pauvre
monastère* as they called it—with little difficulty, and
was welcomed by two of the most charming and
simple of nuns it has ever been my privilege to meet.
They showed me their tiny chapel, where during all
the four years of war they had continued day after
day and night after night to meet together and
chant the Divine Office, in spite of bursting shells
and the fumes of gas. They slept in the cellars, but
kept a little room tidy on the ground floor for what-
ever visitors chanced from time to time to come
and see them. The rest of their monastery, including
the public chapel which adjoined their own choir,

was a mere naked ruin. Nothing could be more striking than the simple fidelity with which these poor nuns clung to their monastic life all through the war, in spite of so much which might legitimately have excused them.

On leaving the Convent I went to our Rear Battalion Headquarters, a small house, still furnished, in the Rue St Maurice, where our Assistant Adjutant lived I found he was out, but I got lunch there, and during it one of the Signallers came in and offered to play the piano for me. He played quite well all through lunch and for half an hour afterwards tunes of every description from rag-time to Gounod. Then I made my way back under the boiling sun along the straight *pavé* road to Aubrey Camp. I used to say Mass here on weekdays in a Nissen hut in the camp, but on Sunday and on the Feast of the Assumption, after saying Mass for the 8th Liverpools whose camp adjoined ours, I had Mass for the Munsters in a long shed open at the sides which had originally been made for horse-standings. It formed now an excellent church, screened from observation by the avenue of tall trees bounding the road, and at the same time delightfully cool. One night, however, the Huns' long hand reached as far back as our own camp, and a burst of high velocity shells forced us to evacuate our huts and move off to a flank. It was on this occasion that a certain well-known old soldier in the battalion, a trifle the worse for drink, made his way up to the Colonel, shook him warmly by the hand, and exclaimed, "There's only one man here, sir, madder than myself, and that's you."

'In the early morning of Sunday, 18th August, we marched away from Aubrey Camp, played out by the pipers of the 1/7 Black Watch who had relieved us the preceding evening. We marched to an entraining point, " Artillery Corner," near Anzin-St-Aubin, and proceeded by light railway to Frevillers, about midway between Arras and St Pol The journey in open trucks on that bright sunny morning was far from unpleasant. We passed on the way, at the foot of the famous tower of St Eloi, a gaunt, white stone ruin perched on the summit of a hill, and visible for miles around. On fine days we used often to see it plainly during the fighting round Cambrai.

We got into Frevillers about eleven o'clock in the morning, and set about as usual to make ourselves as comfortable as the little village would allow.

CHAPTER III

(1) *Hendecourt and Riencourt.*

WE arrived at Frevillers on a Sunday. By Wednesday
I had been my usual rounds, visiting the other two
Battalions and also the Machine Gun Corps, and had
found out from the local Curés the times of Sunday
Mass. That afternoon I wrote out my "notices,"
intending to send them next morning to Division and
Brigade. At dinner, however, I heard that we should
probably be moving in a day or so, and, as I went to
bed, I quite anticipated that the arrangements I had
made would probably be to no purpose.

I had barely settled down in bed when I was
startled by an unusual bugle call. The "Last Post,"
"Lights Out" had long since been sounded—what
could this be? I heard men shouting outside and
fancied that perhaps a fire had broken out. I slipped
on my gum-boots and British warm and went out
into the road. Men were already hurrying up and
down What was afoot—were we moving? Yes,
the answer came back—moving at once and in Battle
Order. I hurried back to my room, and as I was
hastily dressing my servant came in to pack my

valise. It was about eleven o'clock. By midnight we were marching away from Frevillers, out into the darkness and the unknown. That hasty midnight move will always dwell in my mind as a fitting opening for the coming days and nights, filled as these were to be with constant moving—mostly by night—from one shattered battlefield to another, constant fighting, and the almost daily toll of death. At Frevillers nothing more serious than a few articles of kit—forgotten in the hurry—were left behind. All our subsequent moves forward, over the vast Cambrai battlefields, could be traced by Munster graves by Henin, Queant, Fontaine-Notre-Dame, Cantaing, and right up to the very outskirts of the city itself, the last resting-places of those who fell and whom we left, in others' keeping, on each stage of our forward journey.

For the moment, however, our immediate future held nothing more formidable than incessant marching and counter-marching. Our first halting-place was Noyelles-Vion, which we reached as day was breaking. We stayed the whole day there, and I remember the large numbers who came to the Rosary and went to Confession that evening in the beautiful old village church. Late that night we moved off to Gouves near Doullens, passing on our way, as the first faint streaks of dawn were lighting up the sky, through the old mediæval-looking town of Lucheux, which I had known in 1916. At Gouves much the same process was gone through as at Noyelles-Vion, a few hours' sleep in the morning, a fixing up of billets in the hope of a night's rest—one could often rearrange to advantage the original allotment—a lazy afternoon

—this time, I remember, improved on by having a bathe in the village stream—Rosary and Confessions again in the evening at the village church, dinner, and the patient awaiting of orders from Brigade. These arrive at last. The Adjutant tears them open, sits back in his chair and exclaims, "I knew it: moving again." Immediately everything is bustle and preparation and we start off once more. A long wearisome night march brought us this time, in the early hours of Saturday morning, 24th August, to Bavincourt. In the evening we learnt to our relief that we were to remain there that night. I made all arrangements for Mass in the morning, and dined contentedly with several other officers in the excellent 6th Corps Club. On being called next morning, however, I learnt from my servant that we were under orders to move at a moment's notice. I said an early Mass, breakfasted, and then prepared for the march. As a matter of fact, we did not move till nearly midday. The preceding evening an officer of the 3rd Division I had met at the Club told me I should meet my brother at Monchy, and so, when the Battalion moved off, I left it to pursue its way and rode on ahead in search of him.

I reached Monchy without difficulty but could see no sign of the Royal Scots. Patient search and inquiry elicited the information that they were in some trenches beyond "Adinfer Wood," and there at length I found them. My brother was not there at the time, but was expected up that afternoon ; and, talking to the officers, I learnt that the Royal Scots had been already twice engaged in the recent fighting and were expecting to go in again, and that the main difficulty encountered in the advance was from German machine-gun fire, which was responsible for most of our casualties. At length my brother arrived, and we walked back together to Ransart—the destination of the Munsters—had tea there and a long chat, and then parted.

Ransart was a mere heap of ruins and our home an open field. Battalion Headquarters, it is true, took refuge in one of those little two-roomed cottages —such as I had seen at Foncquevillers—built by the French civilians after the German retirement and abandoned during the recent advance. Some of the company officers occupied old dug-outs in a sunken road, but most of the men were just lying out in the open under ground-sheets. Such being the position, it was inevitable that it should rain. It did rain heavily all through the night. The morning broke wet and stormy. I had arranged to say Mass in the open field at nine, and the weather cleared sufficiently for me to begin; but after the Elevation the rain began once more and persisted in a steady downpour, through the General Absolution, the Communion and final prayers, right to the end. In spite of all, however, it was a most consoling Mass, the last, unfortunately, for many there; and as I look back on it now and realise what lay in front of us, there seems to have been a certain fitness in the weeping skies and rain-swept altar.

In the afternoon the silliest thing happened. We found next our Headquarters a wooden box filled with honey and also alive with bees. The problem was to get the bees away and secure the honey, and the only solution which presented itself to the wild lad who acted as our Mess-waiter was to set the whole box alight. Of course he effectually dislodged the bees, and succeeded at the same time in destroying most of the honey. We did, however, manage to save a little.

That same evening about midnight—after a few hours' brief and disturbed sleep—we moved up to Ficheux We spent Tuesday here, and the South Lancs. being next us, I managed to get some of the Catholics together for a few minutes that afternoon. In the evening we moved up towards the line, via Mercatel and Neuville-Vitasse. The latter village was, we understood, to be our destination; but to our surprise we passed on, and continued moving slowly forward till the gathering darkness entirely enveloped us. At length the column halted, and we in rear, knowing nothing of what was passing in front, sat by the roadside and waited. At first I stood, then I sat down, then I stood up again to keep from falling asleep; not that that mattered, but that it meant waking up again and experiencing that hateful sensation when, between sleeping and waking, one only dimly realises the situation. At length my patience was exhausted, and the Doctor and I endeavoured to make our way to the head of the column. We found the road bent sharply to the left, and in the bend, and for half a mile or so beyond it, I don't think I ever remember seeing so complete and absolute a congestion of traffic. The road was a sunken one, allowing no expansion to right or left, and, in the narrow passage, infantry were trying to move forward with their transport, artillery limbers were trying to move back and there they were, all

wedged together, immobile in the darkness. I found
the Colonel and Adjutant seated high up on the bank,
and learnt definitely that we were going to attack
to-morrow about midday. Bully-beef and some
bread and cheese were produced from our mess-cart
and doled out by candle-light; and there we waited
till a rising moon lifted the darkness, and the medley
of traffic gradually melted away. At length we too
moved forward, and turning sharply to the right,
advanced over an open track towards our positions
in the line. On we marched, over the crest of the
hill, till the German "Very" lights flaring up on our
immediate left seemed only a few hundred yards
away. At length we came to a cross-roads, and here
the Colonel stood directing one Company slightly
forward, and turning the other three and Headquarters up the road to the left. We had reached
our positions, and Battalion Headquarters was located
in a shattered German pill-box, where we spent a
few troubled hours endeavouring to sleep in the
cramped enclosure. In the morning the Doctor and
I walked towards Heninel in a vain endeavour to
find the Advanced Dressing Station, and coming back
could not but admire the way in which, though shells
were bursting all around them, our gunners stood by
their guns.

As far as I can remember our bombardment opened
about midday. Long since our pill-box, so lonely
the night before, had been thronged by officers of
all kinds, eagerly waiting to watch the progress of
the fight. The Brigadier and his Brigade-Major were
there, two or three artillery officers, and some
Machine Gunners; and as soon as our barrage opened

and the battle began they all crowded on and around
the pill-box, searching the horizon with their field-
glasses. Suddenly there was a whizz behind us,
followed by a terrific explosion, and a precipitate rush
for cover. However, this was no German shell, but
—it had occurred earlier once before—one of our
heavies dropping short. The Brigadier abandoned
his coign of vantage and his telescope, and rushed
to the telephone to get into communication with the
Artillery Group Headquarters   The two gunner
officers themselves, protesting the entire and obvious
innocence of their own two batteries, hurried away
to put matters right, and then gradually the remainder
of the party re-emerged to watch the progress of the
real fight, undisturbed this time, except for one more
hasty retreat due to the same cause. And all the
while, in front of the keen, eager faces of the watching
group, lay unnoticed the bodies of some who had
fallen during the preceding days, undisturbed now
by the tumult around them, and pointing, one of
them, with mute rigid fingers to the sky.

The objectives of that day's attack were the
villages of Hendecourt and Riencourt. The South
Lancs. and the Kings were to open the advance, and
the Munsters were then to pass through them. The
Battalion had moved forward not long after midday,
but it was not till about two o'clock that Battalion
Headquarters was moved forward and finally established in a pill-box in the Hindenburg Line, a little
to the north of Croisilles. Here we opened a
temporary Aid Post and saw to the first wounded.
It was far from pleasant, as the enemy was deluging
the area with high explosives and gas. Meanwhile,

the Colonel went forward to try and establish his Headquarters somewhere east of the Croisilles-Fontaine-les-Croisilles road, and about four P.M we received orders to move up and join him. This we did painfully and laboriously, and eventually the Doctor and I reached the Aid Post of the 9th Kings practically adjoining the Headquarters. The Doctor here was preparing to move forward, so we carried on his work. The wounded were arriving in constant streams, and the work of evacuating them back to the Advanced Dressing Station was very difficult and slow To add to our difficulties the whole place was being swept by machine-gun bullets. In about an hour, for reasons connected with the fortune of the fight, the Doctor of the 9th Kings returned, and we received orders to return to the Headquarters we had so recently left. This we managed to do just before it got dark, and later that night the whole of the Brigade was withdrawn, and we made our way back to the Transport Lines near St Martin-sur-Cojeuil. In the main, though Croisilles and, I think, Bullecourt were captured that day, this first attack had not been successful, for Hendecourt and Riencourt remained in German hands.

(2) *The Drocourt-Queant Line.*

The next few days were spent in resting and refitting. It was a Thursday morning when we returned to our Transport Lines. That same evening we changed our quarters, moving into the Hindenburg Line just east of St Martin-sur-Cojeuil, and a few miles south of the dominating eminence of Monchy, which had overlooked us so badly when

we lay north of it, still in German hands, by Arras.
Friday and Saturday we spent in the same place,
and I managed during this time to see some of my
Catholics in the 9th Kings, whom so far I had not
had an opportunity of visiting since the fighting
began.

We met together in the middle of an open field
adjoining their camp, and I gave them a General
Absolution and Holy Communion.   On Saturday I
was busy all through the evening hearing Confessions,
and on Sunday morning I said Mass in the trenches
for the Battalion.   Meanwhile, the other Brigades of
the Division had pushed forward the attack we had
begun on 28th August, and had succeeded, though
not without heavy casualties, in capturing the two
villages of Hendecourt and Riencourt.

That same Sunday evening, 1st September, we
moved up the line once more.   We remained a few
hours in the Hindenburg Line just west of Croisilles-
Fontaine-les-Croisilles road, and I was able, whilst
we waited, to hear several more Confessions

Then about midnight we went forward again,
turned off left when we got to the road, went
through the ruins of Fontaine, and halted just outside some dug-outs and trenches.   As on previous
occasions the Doctor and I were together, and we
both slept down in a tiny shanty at the mouth of
an already overcrowded dug-out to snatch a few
hours of troubled, uncertain sleep.

The morning's battle was to be nothing else than
the smashing of the famous Drocourt-Queant Line,
a trench system linking up, from behind, an angle in
the Hindenburg Line.   The plan of attack simply

\

put was this.   The Canadians were to attack the line frontally, pass forward, and capture the village of Cagnicourt.   We were to follow immediately behind, and as soon as the line was passed by the Canadians we were to make a right turn and work down the trench, clearing up the enemy who remained, and consolidating the new position.   The barrage was to open at five A.M.

About half-past four we prepared to move off. Battalion Headquarters personnel were to make immediately for a prominent piece of rising ground known as "The Crow's Nest," just east of Hendecourt Château.   The Doctor and I with the medical staff made for a small trench lying just west of Hendecourt village, where we were to establish the Aid Post.   Dawn was just breaking as we started, and a glance at my watch showed me we had barely ten minutes to reach our trench before the attack would begin.   Our way lay across an open track, but the men being burdened with stretchers and other medical impedimenta, our progress was very slow. I was just beginning to discern our trench a couple of hundred yards away, running at right angles to the track, when our barrage opened.   For a moment we were deafened by the roar of our own guns. Then almost simultaneously the enemy retaliated, and three shells burst in quick succession barely twenty yards in front of us, right on the track Nothing was to be gained by delaying ; we could do nothing but press on as quickly as possible, and happily the next few shells fell on our right and left.   We all tumbled into the trench at last, and hastily moved up it, only to remember we should

have turned left instead of right, which meant re-
tracing our steps along the trench, crossing the open
road and going along the trench beyond, with shells
falling constantly around us. Finally, we came to a
disused mine shaft, where a dug-out had been com-
menced but not finished, and there we set up our
Aid Post; as a matter-of-fact there turned out to be
little need for it there, as nearly all our wounded
passed into a Canadian Collecting Station which
established itself early that morning just in front of us.

As the day grew brighter the scene that morning
became really wonderful. The 63rd or Naval
Division was to pass through us and the Canadians,
and push forward the attack beyond. By six A.M. I
could see them streaming forward over the crest of
the hill behind us by Fontaine-les-Croisilles, innumerable trickles of men they seemed, advancing
everywhere in single file from every corner of the
horizon; and then the guns—there was a battery
next to us we discovered—started to move forward,
followed also by strings of ammunition limbers and
supply wagons; the whole countryside, it seemed,
appeared to be rising up and streaming eastward.
And then in the midst of this universal movement
forward, I could discern little groups at first and
then larger, moving back against the tide—German
prisoners in tens and twenties and hundreds, many
wounded and limping painfully.

The track we had come up that morning became
one of the main routes of evacuation for walking
wounded, as it led directly back to an Advanced
Dressing Station at Fontaine-les-Croisilles. After
seeing to the few of our own wounded who came

our way, there was nothing to do but watch the ever-moving flow of men around us. One figure I shall long remember, an officer of the Naval Division who had been wounded in the head. His wound had been already dressed, and I watched him pass down the road, tall, deadly white, with blood already penetrating his bandage, with his right hand raised to support it, walking steadily forward down that track, a solitary figure, moving out of the roar of battle.

Later in the day the Doctor and I walked over to the Crow's Nest, about twenty minutes' walk away, to find out the news and arrange about moving the Aid Post forward. Hardly any news was then available, but we had hardly got back to our trench before a runner arrived to say that Headquarters were on the point of moving, but he was uncertain where to. I hurried back to the Crow's Nest in the hopes of finding someone there, and of fixing for a guide to be sent back to us, when the new destination should have been fixed. Small things stick in one's mind at times like these, and I well remember as I passed through the ruins of Hendecourt—it comes back to me now, vivid, like a picture—the figure of a dead German soldier lying prostrate on some flag-stones at the foot of a calvary which was still standing at a road junction, within its border of tall trees. On reaching the Crow's Nest I found the place empty, and there was nothing for it but to return again to the Aid Post and wait till morning. We were lucky in getting that night a good sleep, lying on stretchers in the dug-out shaft.

Next morning, after a scanty breakfast—our rations had long since given out, and we lived chiefly on chocolate and salted almonds which had providentially arrived for the Doctor a day or so before—we both set out to look for the new Battalion Headquarters described, by a runner, as being about a thousand yards beyond Riencourt on the Cagnicourt road.

We found them without much difficulty and then went back to guide up the Aid Post personnel. The new Headquarters was in a dug-out actually in that part of the Drocourt-Queant line down which the Battalion had worked the previous morning. Though already cleared, it still bore, in many parts, abundant traces of the fighting. Amongst the litter of dead Germans I remember noticing a young officer lying at the entrance to a dug-out with white socks on and no boots. I imagined him roused from sleep by the opening crash of our bombardment and rushing out in his stockinged feet, though, not unlikely, someone had "souvenired" his boots before I came. How callous men may become in face of death, only war can show. Here were Canadians shaving and brewing tea, completely indifferent to the corpses lying literally at their feet.

That evening we had orders to move. The enemy had been driven right back to the Canal du Nord, and so we formed up on the road and marched away undisturbed in broad daylight over ground which, less than forty-eight hours earlier, had been in German hands.

In spite of severe casualties there was no question as to the complete success of the operation. The Drocourt-Queant Line had gone. We, of course, had our share—perhaps more—in killed and wounded, including three officers killed. Among the latter was another of our company commanders—we had already lost one at Hendecourt—an officer who had served throughout the entire war.

(3) *Inchy and Moeuvres.*

We marched that Tuesday evening, 3rd September, to the famous "Tunnel Trench," a part of the Hindenburg Line lying behind Hendecourt, and so called from a wonderful tunnelled dug-out extending, I believe, for nearly a mile and easily capable of accommodating an entire battalion. It was a place difficult enough to find by day and almost wholly inaccessible by night, so that it was small wonder the ration parties had some difficulty in discovering us, and, in consequence, that we did not sup till two A.M.

The great dug-out was insufferably chill, dusty, and smelly, and next morning everyone sought a home, if only a bivouac sheet above ground. " Tunnel Trench " was in the Hindenburg Support. We moved the Battalion Headquarters into some better accommodation which we found a few hundred yards away in the Hindenburg Front Line, and here we spent four days. On Saturday, 9th September, we had an open-air Mass in the trenches, and that afternoon we moved forward towards the line which now ran between Inchy and Moeuvres facing the Canal du Nord.

For the first few days our Brigade was in "Support," and the Munsters occupied some trenches just south of Cagnicourt. We had an extremely roomy and comfortable dug-out for Battalion Head-quarters, and all the Companies except one had quite

good accommodation   Life here was far from unpleasant, though the walks one took were necessarily
in rather a restive atmosphere, as the enemy shelling,
though seldom concentrated, was extremely widespread, and so one moved in a state of constant
uncertainty as to where he might open next. The
Doctor, for example, went one afternoon with another
officer to the Canteen which the Canadians, with
their habitual resource and promptitude, had already
opened at Cagnicourt.   They found a large queue
waiting outside to be served, and took up their stand
at the end in the hopes of ultimately arriving at the
store.   Their efforts, however, were unavailing, as a 5·9
shell suddenly removed the greater part of the building
before their eyes, and commerce abruptly ceased.
Luckily and strangely enough no one was hurt.

One day I went with Major N—— to reconnoitre
the line which we were to counter-attack if required.
Our walk lay precisely in the insalubrious neighbourhood of Inchy and Moeuvres. All went well till we
were on our way home, when we were imprisoned
for some twenty minutes in a "pill-box," which we
happened on in the nick of time. Our efforts to
leave must have seemed quite ludicrous to the
two Irish Guardsmen who occupied the "pill-box."
Two alternative routes were open to us, one
involving a right turn, the other a left, but, which
ever way we tried, we were invariably driven back
by a shell dropping precisely in our path. Finally,
after several false starts and hasty retreats, we
determined to get away at all costs, and succeeded
in doing so, though from the sounds behind us the
spot remained unsavoury for some time.

On Thursday, 12th September, we relieved the 8th Battalion of the King's Liverpool Regiment in the line between Inchy and Moeuvres. The few days we spent here, from the Thursday till the following Monday night, was one of my worst experiences of trench warfare in France. As the Doctor and I, after walking up together, entered the trenches, the first sight that greeted us was of two huddled forms, partially covered by a ground sheet and pushed away from the duck-boards. They were two of our men who had gone up that morning with the advance party and been killed by a direct hit just outside Battalion Headquarters.

The Aid Post was two or three hundred yards up the trench, and almost each time I passed up and down that little stretch, I could see some fresh sign of shelling, either directly in the trench or on the parapet. Every evening regularly about five o'clock this little segment of line was "hotted" by high explosive and gas, and a direct hit on our "pill-boxes" was by no means uncommon. The Germans had the place "set," as the phrase is, more completely than I ever had known before. One evening, about half-past eight—I had just got back to the Aid Post after dinner—the Adjutant came rushing in to say a man had been badly hit outside the Headquarters. The Doctor and I both hurried back and found the Headquarters "pill-box" filled to suffocation with thick fumes of high explosive, and there in the narrow passage facing the entrance lay poor M'A——, a regimental policeman, who had been on sentry duty outside. His right leg had been completely severed and lay crumpled up underneath him, his right arm was smashed, and he had a gaping wound in his stomach. The Doctor could do little for him, but as he was still conscious, I was able to give him the Last Sacraments. In a short time he lost consciousness and died. The shell had struck the door-post about eighteen inches from the ground, and he had received the full blast of the explosion.

Whilst we were in this sector, one of our isolated posts in front of Moeuvres was attacked about nine P.M. The attack was driven off, leaving two prisoners in our hands. It was renewed again about two hours later and the post was driven back. By morning it was once more in our hands. The skill with which this "minor operation" was arranged and executed at a few hours' notice without, I believe, a single written order being made out, although neighbouring battalions, the artillery, of course, the gunners and trench mortars had all to be warned either to co-operate or to stand by, was to my mind really wonderful, and reflected the greatest credit—though a man of his standing needed none — on our C.O., Lieut.-Col. K——

On the night of 16th September we were relieved by the 5th Battalion of the Highland Light Infantry. The Doctor and I walked back to where our horses were waiting, and rode back in the moonlight through the ruined villages of Pronville and Queant to our camp which was near Bullecourt. We got there about eleven, and it was with immense relief that I followed the Regimental Sergeant-Major to the dug-out that had been allotted me. I saw my valise there waiting for me and a wire bed, and the Mess-waiter

Z

offering me hot tea and bread and jam. Of course the comfort that one appreciated so much was merely relative. It required life in the line as a background to make a bed that was much too short, and a dug-out which smelt earthy and was damp and leaked when the rain came, appear the last word in comfort.

The following afternoon I rode over to Queant to bury M'A——. As I was waiting for the grave to be finished I walked round the cemetery and discovered the names of some English airmen who had crashed in the German lines and whose graves, besides the cross, were marked with fragments of their aeroplanes. I also noticed the graves of some British soldiers who had fallen during the great Cambrai drive of November 1917, and of some Russians, presumably prisoners of war, made to work in the war zone.

On Wednesday, 18th September, the whole Battalion marched away to Boiselles, entrained there and detrained at Beaumetz, on the Arras-Doullens main line. From Beaumetz we marched to billets in the little village of Bailleulmont, arriving about four in the afternoon.

We spent a week here, training in the morning, free in the afternoon ; and for me there was nothing more thrilling than a few rides round the country fixing Mass for the other units, lunch one day at a neighbouring Casualty Clearing Station, and a trip to the Officers' Clothing Depot at Doullens. One day some officers from the 2nd Munsters paid us a visit, and some old friends of Gallipoli days met again , and on another evening the Battalion gave an impromptu concert which was quite amusing and much appreciated, though, as always on the eve of battle, pathetic in the extreme, so brief the hours remaining inevitably to some of those who, on such evenings, are out so whole-heartedly to amuse and be amused.

(4) *Cambrai at last*

On Wednesday, 18th September, we entrained at Beaumetz and went via Arras, Achiet-le-Grand, and Bapaume, to Vaulx-Vraucourt.   Here we detrained and marched to Lagnicourt.   Our home consisted of a bare field on the side of a small valley leading up to Queant   Already the evenings were closing in and the nights growing cold, so that a small supply of tents and bivouac sheets, which arrived about ten P M., was very welcome.   Next morning, as I was walking round the camp, who should appear but my brother whom I had last seen at Ransart.   We were delighted to meet, and after wandering through the ruined village he left me, as he had an appointment at two, but promised to return, if possible, afterwards. This he did and we spent the afternoon together. It would have been wholly pleasant but for the anticipation of the coming conflict, which hung like a dark cloud over our horizon.   My brother left me after tea, and I spent the whole remainder of the evening hearing Confessions, till the cold and the darkness and the lateness of the hour led me to give a General Absolution to those who remained   Then I returned to our tent which served both as a Mess and as a sleeping place.   The others had already finished dinner, so I made a hasty meal and then settled myself to take a few hours' sleep   We were due to move off at 1 30   We were wakened at about

half-past twelve, and I heard the rain pattering down
on to the tent as I gathered up my haversack and gas
mask and prepared to go out into the night.   Outside
it was pitch dark, and it took some time for the whole
Battalion to form up on the road just outside the
camp.   When all were ready to start I took up my
position about the middle of the column, and with
the Colonel standing behind me, gave the General
Absolution to the entire Battalion as it stood there
in the rain and murky darkness on the eve of battle.
Then when I had finished we all joined in saying
the " Our Father."   How well I remember the Colonel
taking up my words and saying, in his loud,
commanding voice, so that all might hear, " Now,
men, we'll say the ' Our Father' together."   Then we
moved away up the road, and as we went we could
hear the cavalry trumpets ringing out reveille.

After going a short distance along the road, we
turned sharply to the right, and climbing up a steep
bank, made our way overland to the assembling positions.   The route seemed interminable, every moment
we were stumbling over shell-holes and slipping down
muddy banks.   At one time we were halted for
about half an hour whilst another battalion crossed
our path.   It was not till nearly dawn that we ultimately rested in the Hindenburg Line—we had
been advancing parallel to it—just south of Inchy.
I went down with the Doctor into a dug-out, ate a
sandwich, and was just preparing to lie down when
we were on the move again.   As we clambered
out of the trench dawn was breaking, and with it
there opened a most tremendous bombardment.   A
Division in front of us was just breaking out of

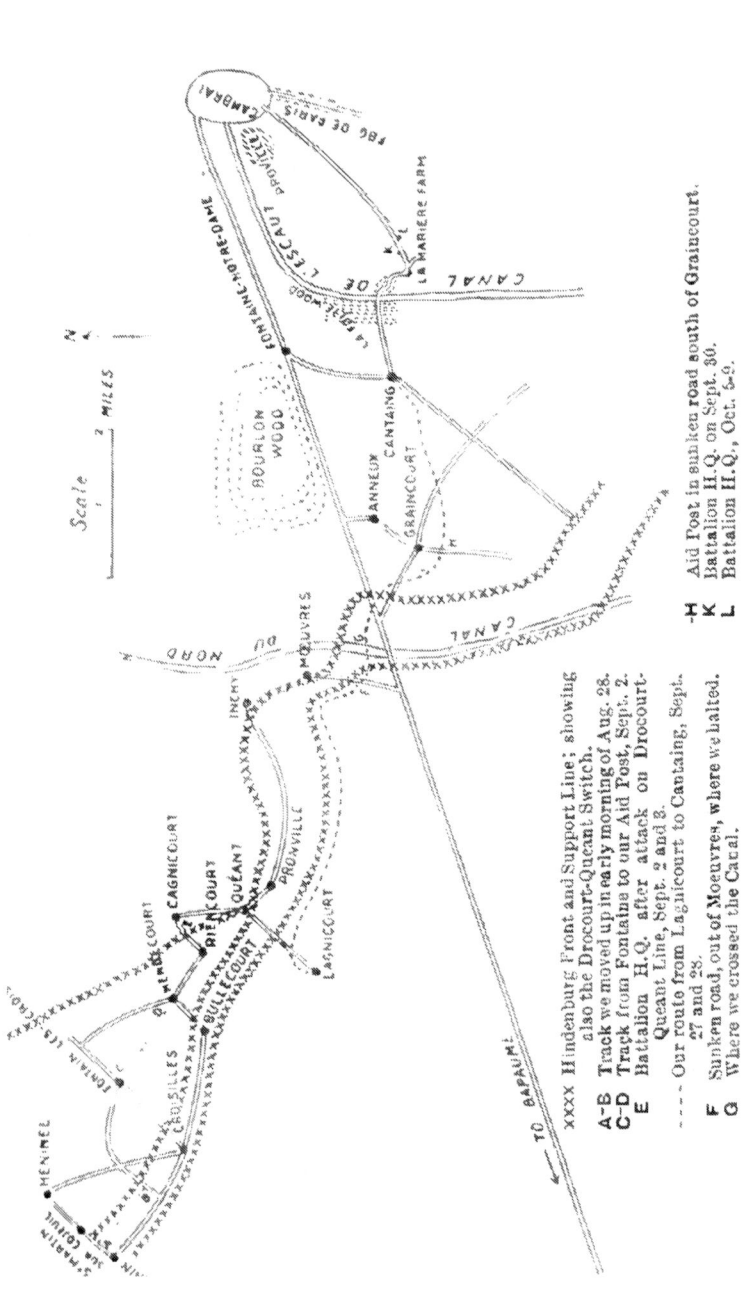

Scale
2 MILES

N

xxxx Hindenburg Front and Support Line; showing
    also the Drocourt-Quéant Switch.
A–B Track we moved up in early morning of Aug. 28.
C–D Track from Fontaine to our Aid Post, Sept. 2.
E   Battalion H.Q. after attack on Drocourt-
     Quéant Line, Sept. 2 and 3.
----- Our route from Lagnicourt to Cantaing, Sept.
       27 and 28.
F   Sunken road, out of Moeuvres, where we halted.
G   Where we crossed the Canal.

H   Aid Post in sunken road south of Graincourt.
K   Battalion H.Q. on Sept. 30.
L   Battalion H.Q., Oct. 6-9.

SKETCH MAP SHOWING STAGES OF OUR ADVANCE ON CAMBRAI.

Moeuvres and advancing to the Canal du Nord. We, too, started almost immediately to walk forward, now in the trench, now out of it. From time to time shells burst near us, and there was a worrying, persistent stream of gas which was rather demoralising; but what worried us most as we descended into the valley running south from Moeuvres, was a mild, desultory machine-gun fire which seemed to come from quite close by. At length we all gained in safety the shelter of a road running down the valley and protected on the east side by a high bank. Shells burst above us on the bank and beyond us in the valley, but only once or twice on the road itself, and here we halted.

We must have waited on this road nearly two hours; then we started forward again over the bank and into a trench. This trench had been captured that morning and bore abundant and horrible traces of the fight. In places it was so choked with dead that we had to get out and walk over the open, and at one point I saw a man with his head as neatly severed as though an axe had done it. The enemy was now withdrawing his guns, and as in every forward movement, there was a brief spell of comparative immunity from hostile shell-fire. As we dipped down over the farther crest of the rise we had been crossing, I heard our Intelligence Officer shouting to me. He was speaking to a tall German officer, and told me how the Colonel and he, going forward to reconnoitre, had come upon a nest of German machine-gunners who had lain concealed in a dug-out when the British first swept over, and had then emerged and opened fire on the troops who were, as we had been, following up. Luckily, the Colonel and his party came on them from behind, and they promptly surrendered, not, however, as I afterwards heard, without having caused us many casualties.

Our next halt was in the Canal du Nord itself, which has never been finished and was still dry. As we waited there several groups of German prisoners passed back. One was so badly wounded that he lay there when his party moved on again, and it was pathetic to see the haunted, pleading look of a pal of his who remained to watch beside him. We left them both there, and as we left the canal, always going east, I saw a wretched German, quite an old-looking man, and wounded, climb painfully out of a dug-out and look hopelessly and helplessly around him. No one heeded him. The last thing I noticed—a common sight in these days—was a German machine-gunner, a young lad he seemed, lying dead with his gun beside him, in position on the lip of the bank.

We took up our next position in a shallow trench only a few hundred yards away from the canal, and here again we waited two or three hours. Lack of information as to the situation in front was holding our Division up. We were, however, comfortable enough till a supporting Division, which was advancing behind ours, appeared and wanted to occupy our line. We were just looking around for a new position when orders came for us to advance, this time in haste and in earnest. The enemy was still in Cantaing and we were to take it. We advanced rapidly over open ground in a south-easterly direction. We were in "artillery formation" *i.e.* in little

groups with Headquarters bringing up the rear. We
ourselves were in three groups, the Colonel, striding
ahead in a mackintosh, was leading one, an officer,
another, and the Orderly-Room Corporal, I remember,
was leading the third, in which the Doctor and I
were. As we advanced the menacing dark masses of
Bourlon Wood loomed up on our left, and in the far
distance, plainly visible in the bright evening light,
there stood out the three towers of Cambrai. I
remember thinking what a wonderful advance it all
was, and how easy it seemed, this walking forward
over open fields, which that very morning had been
in German hands. As we drew near Graincourt,
however, the shell-fire increased considerably and
alarmingly, and machine-gun fire became incessant.
The enemy, evidently, was not far away. Our first
casualty was an officer, wounded in the back, but
not seriously. After attending to him the Doctor
and I pushed forward to a sunken road leading south
from Graincourt, and here, about half a mile from
the village, we set up the Aid Post. Meanwhile, the
attack was being made, and for long hours we stayed
in that sunken road, with a constant stream of
casualties coming through, working there amidst
the wounded in the gathering darkness, surrounded
by the grey faces of the dying and the dead. At the
beginning everything was done in the open, then we
tried to utilise a tiny shaft for dressing stretcher-
cases, and rigged up a prop for one stretcher at a
time, and the Doctor worked there by candle-light.
All lesser cases were treated in the open, and it was
only with the greatest difficulty we managed to stow
some of the worst cases down a deep dug-out we

found there, till the overworked Bearers could get them away.   Luckily, we found several German greatcoats, and these served to cover those of the wounded who had perforce to lie in the open.

About midnight the flow of casualties ceased and we managed to get a few hours' sleep.   Next morning the Doctor and I went forward to get into touch with Battalion Headquarters.   We made our way up a shallow trench and soon came upon the Regimental Sergeant-Major and a few orderlies and servants, in a little shelter dug in beside the trench. This had been Headquarters the night before, and a guide was to be sent back to bring up the remainder as soon as the new Headquarters had been fixed. After a cup of tea the Doctor and I decided to push on, when I was suddenly overcome by an attack of faintness and had to lie down and rest where I was, whilst the Doctor went on alone.   In an hour or two I felt much better, and on the arrival of Lieut. O'N—— and a few men carrying rations forward, and also in search of Battalion Headquarters, I joined on to them and we all went forward together.   I heard then more or less what the situation was.   Apparently, the evening before, our attack had been completely held up by machine-gun fire, to which nearly all our casualties were due.   It was renewed again in the early morning, and this time little opposition was encountered, and we were now well into and beyond the village of Cantaing.   As we walked up that morning by the side of the trench, there before us were the German machine guns and their gunners lying dead beside them.

Finding the way was, however, no easy task, and

2 A

we were almost in despair when we met the guide who was going, as arranged, to bring up the remainder of Headquarters. He had a stretcher-bearer with him, who assured us he knew the way up to where the Battalion was, so we sent the guide on and kept the stretcher-bearer with us. We reached Cantaing without much difficulty, but as we were walking up the main street the enemy started dropping heavy shells in the village; and it was only then that I discovered to my horror that our guide had never been himself to Battalion Headquarters, but had just been told he couldn't miss it if he went up the main street, as there was a green flag outside. We went up almost to the very end of the village, but seeing no sign of any green flag, nor any Munsters about at all, and the shelling continuing to be very unpleasant, we beat a hasty retreat to the farther and apparently safer end of Cantaing. The few soldiers we met here had only the vaguest information to give, but finally, as the shelling abated, we decided to try again, and happily on the way we met Major M'C——, commanding the 2/4 South Lancs., who told us to keep straight on till we came to a big brewery on the left, and that there we should find our Headquarters. This we did, and I saw that we must have been barely a stone's-throw away when we so hastily withdrew before. The green flag *was* there, but almost infinitesimal in size. I think it was a pocket handkerchief.

We found Battalion Headquarters installed in a roomy cellar, with the Mess looking out on to the road, and with an inner room behind fitted up with several beds, and having an exit up some steps into the yard behind. Everyone was in the best of spirits.

but I was surprised to find the Doctor had not yet
arrived.   He did not turn up till the following
morning.   It appeared that, after leaving me, he had
wandered about in a solitary endeavour to find our
Headquarters, and after being several times wrongly
directed, had finally made his way back to where he
had left me.   Finding that the whole party had disappeared he returned to our old Aid Post in the
sunken road, spent the night there with his staff, and
made his way up to Cantaing next morning.

We spent Saturday night at Cantaing and the
whole of Sunday.   The companies were disposed in
front, in dug-outs and trenches on the road to
Fontaine-Notre-Dame.   Early on Monday morning,
30th September, whilst it was still dark the Battalion
moved up towards Cambrai.   The attack that
morning was to be directed against the Faubourg de
Paris, and was worked out on the report and
assumption that the neighbouring suburb of Proville
was already in our hands.   After leaving Cantaing
the Battalion moved straight up, through the edge of
La Folie Wood, to the Canal de L'Escaut, crossed it
at the lock bridge, bore round to the left and then to
the right, mounted straight over the crest of the hill,
and then made for the Faubourg de Paris.   None
reached it that autumn morning.   An intense and
continuous machine-gun barrage, coming from the
direction of Proville, completely paralysed the whole
operation, and the Battalion had to dig in where
it stood.

Meanwhile, the Doctor and I had established the
Aid Post at La Mariere Farm, a big building,
comparatively little damaged, standing at the corner

of the road where it turned north-east towards Cambrai. We had not got there, however, without incident. We had barely left Cantaing before word was brought that the Battalion was suffering heavy casualties from shell-fire, crossing the canal. We went forward from the rear, but in the darkness could find no trace of the wounded. As a matter-of-fact I think they were carried back direct to an A.D.S. on the roadside belonging to the Naval Division. The Doctor then had to go back to see about some of his staff who apparently had got lost, and I went on with the medical Corporal to fix up the Aid Post. The road beyond the canal was littered with broken branches and wounded and dead, and the whole atmosphere was permeated with gas. Where the road mounts the hill there is on the left a wide, deep depression in the ground something like a disused quarry, and there, in fairly good shelter from shells, we awaited the arrival of the Doctor. After some time he at length arrived having, I found, been busy with several casualties on the way up, and together we went into La Mariere Farm, and ultimately established the Aid Post in a cellar. It was some time, however, before we could occupy it, as we found it in possession of some signallers; and so, till we found them another cellar, less convenient for getting stretchers down but otherwise as good as the one they occupied, all the casualties were dressed above ground. As I was looking over the farm to see what accommodation there was, I suddenly, from an open window, came across a wonderful view of the towers of Cambrai about four miles away. They looked beautiful in the early morning light, and

I would have lingered but for the sudden whistle of a bullet which passed through the gaping window out into the yard behind.

All through that long day there was a constant stream of casualties. Early in the afternoon we heard the Colonel had been hit I went out almost at once, up the short stretch of road to a ruined house on the left which served as Battalion Headquarters. The road was awful, beyond description, strewn with dead men and animals, and the first sight that greeted me as I entered the building was the huddled, crumpled form of a dead soldier just killed. I penetrated a few hundred yards out into the open field on the right, and crouching down to take cover from the bullets found I was lying next to a dead machine-gun officer. When I saw the Colonel ultimately, he was quite unconscious and obviously dying. I gave him the Last Sacraments, and he was taken away.

That night the Battalion was relieved. The Doctor and I decided to pass the night where we were in case further casualties came in. We had that evening a German prisoner, brought in badly wounded, and though the Doctor did everything for him, it soon became evident he was dying and so not worth sending away So there he lay on the stretcher, breathing out his last and swinging his arms about wildly in his death agony, while around him, quite unmoved, our men continued their preparation for supper, making tea and stewing meat. So at length he died, a lonely, pathetic figure. He was just twenty years old.

Next morning, 1st October, the Doctor and I set

out to join the Battalion in La Folie Wood. It
was a lovely autumn morning, and for once the
wood seemed beautiful in spite of its shattered trees
and the heavy oppressive smell of gas which clung
persistently around it. After much wandering over
broken paths and through tangled undergrowth, we
at length found the clearing where the Battalion was
encamped. Our Mess was in one of the Lodge
Houses—what was left of it—and I had my fiist
shave and wash for two days and a good breakfast
and felt much refreshed. The Doctor and I fixed
up our home in a "pill-box" in the wood, which
already housed the officers of two of the companies.
We slept there to the number of nine—seven in
bunks, one bunk being made to hold two, and two
on the floor, one being a machine-gun officer of
another Division whose guns were manning the
canal bank.

Whilst we were in the wood I arranged to hear
Confessions every evening at six in one of the men's
shelters. The first evening I had barely started
when our guns—several batteries of which lined
the western fringe of the wood—opened a terrific
bombardment which lasted fully an hour. I don't
think I ever heard so continuous and deafening a
roar. Of course, being just in front of the guns,
and living in a wood which caught and held the
volume of noise, the sound was intensified. It
was absolutely bewildering, and, though growing in
volume every evening, it continued more or less un-
interruptedly throughout the day, and had a most
unsteadying influence on everybody and stretched
one's nerves to breaking point. The whole period

was a most trying one. We lost our Transport
Officer, killed direct as he was walking up one morning to the camp, by a falling bullet fired at an
aeroplane. The Brigadier and Brigade-Major were
both badly wounded. They, and several of our own
officers, had shelters in a sunken lane right under
the muzzles of the line of guns. These were
constantly drawing heavy enemy fire, and one day,
several shells falling short, dropped right into the
lane, causing heavy casualties.

I remember, as I was wondering where precisely
they were dropping and whether any harm was
being done, in rushed an officer, who had himself
just escaped from the lane, telling several of us who
were grouped round the " pill-box " that the Brigadier
had been hit. Then, as if shelling by day was not
enough, we were harassed at night by bombs. We
ourselves escaped untouched, but the South Lancs.
next us had several casualties, killed and wounded.

One afternoon I went over to Cantaing to bury
ten of our men and one unknown soldier who had
been brought down from across the canal. It was
gruesome and unpleasant work, as several had been
badly wounded and were lying stiff and stark in all
sorts of unnatural attitudes.

We remained in our camp till Friday, 4th October,
when the Battalion took up a defensive line on the
west bank of the canal, with one Company thrown
forward into Proville, which had at length passed into
British hands. On Saturday night, however, there was
a complete *volte-face*, and we had sudden orders, late
that evening, to withdraw from our actual positions
and take up a new one in the front line just south-

west of Cambrai, and facing the Faubourg de Paris,
which the enemy still held.

Everything, as usual, had to be done in darkness.
It was with considerable difficulty that the Battalion
was ultimately got together, and it was not till
midnight that we marched out down the western
side of La Folie Wood. Our route lay once more
over the bridge by the lockgates.   I don't think
I ever hated a stretch of road or feared one so much
as this.   It was fœtid with the smell of dead men
and horses, and the fumes of gas which clung about
the trees.   It was, moreover—especially the crossing
by the bridge—subjected to constant shell-fire.   Once
again we had to trudge along it, but this time happily
we did so without casualties, except for one man
who, in the press of traffic, fell into the canal, and
was with difficulty rescued half dead with cold.   At
length we reached the road leading from La Mariere
Farm towards Cambrai.   Here we had to wait an
interminable time, till the outgoing Battalion—the
same which had relieved us in the line by Inchy and
Moeuvres—had painfully clambered out of the tiny
entrance of the Headquarters' dug-out, and so made
room for our own men to enter.

The Headquarters' dug-out had in reality three
entrances, though only one led out into a trench and
so to the road.   Of these entrances one was an
ordinary shaft with steps; the other two were
obstructed at the top by small "pill-boxes" built
over the entrance.   Here it was necessary, after
ascending the stairs, to mount a dozen steps or so
of a perpendicular iron ladder let into the concrete,
turn sharply to the left and then to the right down

a tiny passage about four feet high and two and a half feet wide. Naturally, the process of getting several men out that way took time, but we did at length manage to squeeze ourselves down into the main room of the dug-out. I learnt here to my regret that the Doctor, a charming young Scotsman from Glasgow, who had taken over our Aid Post in the Inchy-Moeuvres sector, had been killed the following day.

Our home for the moment, where six officers used to live and sleep and one signaller to operate, was about twelve feet long and three feet wide. It had a table and one chair. If life was far from comfortable we were yet the cheeriest of parties, and I for one slept quite well, even though from time to time the signaller did step unavoidably on my face. One unusual incident occurred whilst I was here. Two of our men were killed in the trench behind us by a direct hit on their shelter. I was burying the poor, mangled remains next morning when who should come round the traverse but an official photographer, who took quite a good photograph as the little service was proceeding.

Another memory of these days was the wonderful view we got at nights of Cambrai in flames. The fires seemed to be chiefly at the eastern extremity of the town, as the three tall towers—marking the city's principal churches—used to stand out in bold relief against the lurid background of flame.

Whilst we were here we had what was for me the worst experience of gas during the war. A gas shell landed in two of our three entrances, whilst several others fell round about. The dug-out, where we all were at the time, was immediately filled with the suffocating fumes. We put on our gas masks hoping it would soon clear. After nearly half an hour, during which we got some of the men out of the dug-out, so as to allow a freer current of air, the Doctor took a sniff and instantly put on his mask again; the gas was still thick, and there was nothing for it but to get right out into the open. The climb up the sixty or seventy steep steps was a most exhausting operation, and most of us had to stop half-way to get breath, so quickly and so deeply had the gas already affected us. I know I had the greatest difficulty in getting out into the open, and once there, I tore off my mask, heedless as to whether the atmosphere was good or bad. Happily it was all right, but it was several hours before the dug-out itself was free.

On Tuesday, 9th October, there was a renewed attack on Cambrai. The 24th Division, I think it was, attacked round the city on the south, and our Division covered their flank. Our own Battalion had nothing further to do than throw out a screen of smoke bombs. The Faubourg de Paris, however, remained in enemy hands till late that evening, as the usual harassing machine-gun fire played over our Headquarters that night. At 1.30 next morning the Canadians attacked round the north of the city, and by dawn, Cambrai was in British hands at last. The 57th Division, holding, as we had done, the line in front of the city, sent in patrols at once, and amongst the first to enter were the Munsters. In the afternoon I went in myself and saw something of the town. I visited the Cathedral and its sacristy, rifled by the Germans, met the French priest who had stayed in the city in spite of the order evacuating civilians, and went over a big Convent or Seminary, I am not sure which, near the Cathedral and used by the Germans as a hospital. It contained a very pretty Chapel, which we found strewn with wood shavings, I fancy, to lay the wounded on as they arrived. I then walked back by a road which only a few hours previously had been almost impassable owing to enemy machine-gun fire.

There seems a sort of instinct which tells a soldier when danger has gone. That Wednesday morning, though there was nothing official about the evacuation of Cambrai or the Faubourg de Paris, everyone had started walking about openly over ground which, the night before, had been swept by bullets. It had seemed quite strange to watch one of our Company Commanders, a very tall soldier, come striding towards us from his Headquarters right across the open instead of following the trench. And now here was I walking back in the evening with not a shot being fired and no sound of guns.

We took the opportunity of this sudden change to fix the exact spot where the Colonel had been hit—we found his steel helmet still lying there—and to mark it with white stones. We also collected several of our own dead lying around, and had them brought back to Fontaine-Notre-Dame where they were buried.

At seven that night we marched back to our Transport Lines near Fontaine-Notre-Dame, and the following morning, Thursday, 10th October, we marched down the main Cambrai-Bapaume road, and camped in an open field about a mile south of Inchy, pitching our tents on ground where ten days previously no one could have shown himself with safety. The same evening Lieutenant-Colonel L—— joined us and took command of the Battalion.

On Friday I bicycled over to Hermies and met my brother again. We celebrated our safe survival from the fight in an excellent lunch in the same 6th Corps Club, which I had last seen at Bavincourt. We had tea in my brother's Mess, and then, after listening for a few minutes to their Pipers, I bicycled back. We were to move the following day.

CHAPTER IV

LILLE

WE left our camp at Inchy on the afternoon of Saturday, 12th October. We were to entrain about half-past five, and had timed our march so as to arrive at the entraining point about four in order that the men might have tea before starting. After tea we heard that our train would be late. Of station, of course, there was no sign, merely, in the valley below us, was a single line of railway and a few sidings. There was nothing for it but to resign ourselves—after a " tot " of rum provided by a provident Quartermaster—to spend the time as cheerfully as we could on that bleak hill-side, in spite of the dark and the cold

The train arrived at last, and by half-past seven, after the usual disputes with other units accused of occupying too many trucks and the inevitable efforts to crowd a seemingly impossible number of men into an already overcrowded wagon, we finally started. We found ourselves—about six of us with the Colonel—in an evil-smelling dirty truck. However, I had travelled in France too often during the war to have expected anything different. As a matter-of-fact, with a valise to sit on and a blanket, one can really spend a far more comfortable night in a moderately clean horse-box, than in a dilapidated second-class carriage innocent alike of cushions on the seats or glass in the windows. One can at least stretch one's legs or lie down at full length without entangling oneself in other people.

This particular journey was, however, unusually unpleasant. To start with, the floor of the truck was grimy and dirty, we had no blankets, in fact nothing warmer than mackintoshes, and it was extremely cold. Moreover, it took us till eleven o'clock on Sunday morning to reach Béthune, where we were to detrain.

We had left Hermies under the blissful delusion that we were out for a week's rest, and it was well that the worst of the journey was over before the illusion was dispelled. It transpired, as we marched from Béthune to our billets at Vaudricourt, that we were going to move again next day. Vaudricourt was quite a pleasant village and the billets were excellent, but we had to leave it next morning early and march to Verquin, the adjoining village, where we were to embus. An alarmingly early start—I think we breakfasted about seven—did not by any means imply an early departure from Verquin. We hung about this village, though the buses were there in front of us and the men sitting in them, for two or three hours, and it was eleven o'clock before we actually started. Our route lay through Béthune and Locon, and then we turned to the right and finally debussed at the Pont du Hem on the Estaires-La Bassée road.

A long march brought us to our final destination, a camp at Le Touquet north-east of the village of

Fromelles and near Le Maisnil-en-Weppes. In spite of all the surrounding desolation there was a certain interest in the locality. One of our Companies had its Headquarters in a " pill-box" which before must have been almost in the old German front line, a few hundred yards away from the Le Bridoux salient where I had watched the aeroplane come down in flames last summer. One could see at a glance how much better off the Germans had been when holding this sector than ourselves. Their " pill-boxes," practically unknown on our side, were everywhere, and some almost in the front line, and once inside these, one could defy any barrage

We left our camp on Wednesday afternoon, 16th October, and marched to Radinghem. Battalion Headquarters was set up in a tiny half-ruined " pill-box" already occupied by some wireless operators, and the Companies were in trenches and shelters round about. After having spent a few most cold and uncomfortable hours here, we moved off at 2.30 next morning towards Lille, via the Château de Flandre outside the village, and then on towards a little group of houses on the Lille road, which went by the ironical name of Fin de la Guerre.

The preceding evening the enemy had dropped several shells round about Radinghem, causing heavy casualties, in particular at the cross-roads near the Château de Flandre. Now, however, as we moved up in the dark that Thursday morning, a strange stillness brooded over the whole country-side. The ill-omened cross-roads were passed in safety, and not a shot broke the stillness of the night as we waited outside the Château for our guides.

Fin de la Guerre became our temporary Headquarters, and we stayed there till about nine o'clock,
when we moved forward once more and established
ourselves at Vert Ballot, near the village of Englos,
with the Companies as usual disposed in front.   Our
new Headquarters was in quite a roomy and
moderately intact house, part of which had been
converted into a " pill-box."   Our only dread was
of hidden mines and booby-traps.   As we were
leaving our old Headquarters at Fin de la Guerre a
party of R.E. Tunnelling Company, whose unpleasant
task it was to discover and destroy these traps,
declared *that* house unsafe; and we had barely
arrived at Vert Ballot before an enormous explosion
a few hundred yards away warned us that this sort of
hidden danger lay about everywhere and in every
shape.   On this occasion the two men engaged in
investigating this particular contrivance were killed
on the spot, being literally blown to pieces.   Needless to say, aided by an R.E. Corporal attached to
us for the purpose, we subjected our own house to a
rigorous search.   Here we found nothing, but the
Corporal produced the finished article from another
house where one of the Companies lived—a long
board with some twenty stick bombs attached and
connected up by wire, and made ready for action by
a slow burning fuse and detonator.

That afternoon I went round with the Adjutant to
the little village of Hallenes, to get into touch with
another Battalion of the Brigade which was supposed
to be there.   In the course of our walk we came
upon the dead body of a Highlander in kilts, lying
in a barn.   He had been shot through the forehead

with a revolver, while forming part no doubt of a
forward patrol; but what struck me most of all,
through that short autumn afternoon, was the un-
canny stillness everywhere—not a sound of battle,
and, on all sides, houses, not in ruins, as of old, but
just silent and empty.

We returned to our Headquarters and spent there
a very comfortable night. Next day, 18th October,
(Friday), we marched into billets at Le Marais just
west of Lille. Here we were extremely well off,
with any number of good, furnished houses to choose
from, and a fine Church which proved most useful
in the evenings and on Sunday.

The evacuation of civilians from this area had
only been ordered a few days before, and the German
notices ordering the evacuation and summoning all
males from fifteen to fifty years of age to present
themselves at the Commandant's office in Lille, were
still on the walls. The Germans themselves, as the
state of the houses showed, had only left a few
hours previously. Drawers had been opened and
their contents littered the floors, and needless to
say, everything valuable and easily portable had
been carried off. A vigorous cleaning up, however,
sufficed to make our billets quite comfortable.
Whilst we were at Le Marais the Battalion provided
a Guard of Honour of a hundred men for President
Poincaré, on his first visit to Lille since its liberation.
The smartness and physique of the men were much
commented on.

On Monday, 21st October, the Battalion marched
to billets at Ascq, about six miles east of Lille.
Our march through Lille was a regular triumphal

2 ʳ

procession. In spite of the early hour, seven o'clock, crowds soon gathered around, shaking hands with the men, clapping and cheering, and offering us flowers and flags,' so that by the time we reached Ascq the Battalion was a mass of colour.

After one night at Ascq we marched to Willems, a village almost on the Belgian frontier, and remained there till Thursday. Everywhere we heard the same tale from the civilians of the brutality and aggressive insolence of the Germans during their four years' domination—constant requisitions, constant fines and imprisonment, the arrest of prominent men and women, and the carrying them off to German prisons, the preaching even from the pulpit of the morality of looting, provided it was from the helpless French civilian — such was the constant burden of their conversation with us. The Curé at Willems told me that, barely a fortnight before the German evacuation, he had been given twenty-four hours to clear completely out of his house as it was required by the military authorities, and, when I met him, he was still living in the house where he had found hospitality.

On Thursday we moved up to Le Cornet, just inside the Belgian frontier, and Battalion Head-quarters was established at " Hardy Planck " Farm. The two other Brigades of our Division had been holding the line during the last few days, and our Brigade was now relieving one of these. One Battalion was in the front line facing Tournai, one round Honnevain, and the third at Le Cornet " Hardy Planck " Farm had originally been built as a " place-forte " in 1556, and was a most interesting

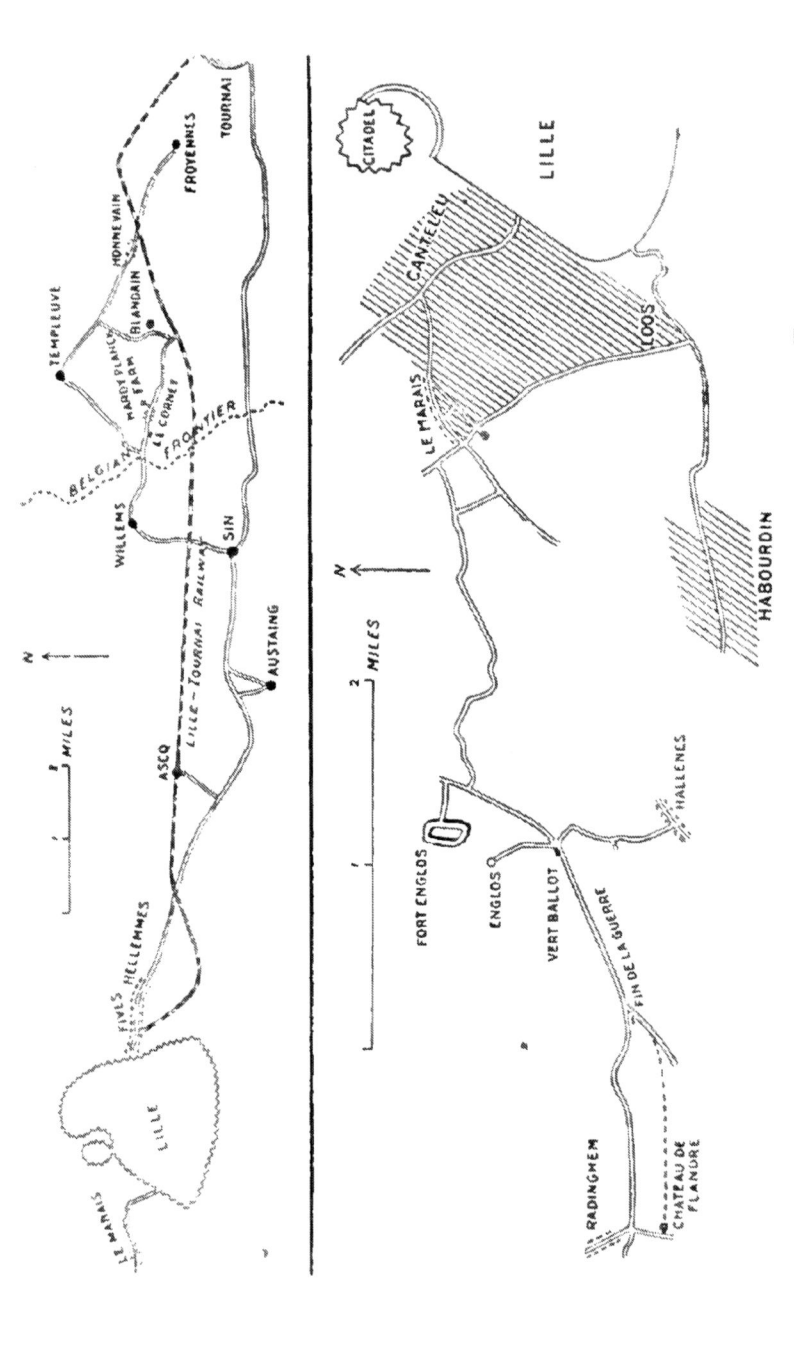

SKETCH MAPS SHOWING STAGES OF OUR ADVANCE TOWARDS TOURNAI.

and picturesque old place. Part of the moat was
still remaining, and the room the Colonel occupied—
a small vaulted chamber — had the appearance of
originally being the Chapel. The Mess was a big
stone-floored, oak-ceilinged room with what once had
been a magnificent open fire-place, now filled in
and replaced by an ordinary French stove. There
were several other similar rooms both on the ground
floor and above. The capacious cellars — partly
below the level of the moat—were filled with refugees,
mostly from Blandain, a village which was at times
subjected to rather heavy shelling. Not a little
shelling took place also round Le Cornet, the roads
and cross-roads, rather than the houses, being
especially singled out for attention. The enemy
as usual contrived to have perfect observation of
the whole country from Mont Aubert, north of
Tournai, plainly visible to us with its white Church
on top.

Much of the Doctor's time here was taken up in
visiting civilian sick. , There seemed to be quantities
about, and once it became known we had a *médecin*
with us, his services, in spite of two deaths, were
in constant demand. I acted mostly as interpreter,
except in one case where I gave the Last Sacraments
to a dying old woman.

Much excitement was caused at this time by our
capture of a reputed spy. It was natural that the
Germans should have left many agents behind them
when they withdrew ; and so when a man passing down
the road was pointed out by civilians as *bosche et espion*
the trail was worth taking up. An officer, accompanied by the soldier to whom the information had

been given, spent almost an entire day tracking their
man down. At length they cornered him in his
own house—which seemed to contain nothing more
suspicious than rather large supplies of foodstuffs—
and brought him along to Headquarters. He was
a typical Flemish peasant, with nothing very desperate
in his appearance, but the united witness of the
civil population counselled his detention. Acting on
instructions from Brigade we kept him that night,
and handed him over to the Military Police in the
morning He was lodged in a cellar with a sentry
on the door, and when we went to see him after
dinner he made a great moan about the cold,
constantly repeating " Je suis malheureux, vous
savez"; but since he had plenty of straw to lie on,
which was more than many of our men had, I don't
think he had really much to complain of. We heard
no more about him, but the rumour naturally was
that he was sentenced to death.

We left our comfortable quarters at " Hardy
Planck " Farm on Monday, 28th October, and moved
up to Honnevain, the Battalion we took over from
there going up to the front line, and the one there
taking our place at Le Cornet. Honnevain proved
hardly less agreeable than the billets we had just
left. Battalion Headquarters and three of the
Companies were all billeted in houses, one Company
was thrown forward across the railway line, and
occupied a brick kiln and some trenches about midway between Honnevain and the front line system
round Froyennes

There were still some civilians left at Honnevain,
and I remember in particular one dear old lady

whose house we thought of occupying. She was full of a quiet dignity, but at the same time pained, puzzled and, I think, not a little alarmed at our entry, which was certainly somewhat abrupt. We had found the front gate closed, and thinking the house unoccupied, easily overcame that obstacle. The front door was also closed, but undoing one of the window shutters we saw through the broken glass, just what we were looking for, several wooden beds left by the Germans   Whilst one of the officers was trying to get through the window, I noticed a side door and finding it open, walked in. The others followed, and we were just beginning to explore the house when, turning round, I found myself face to face with an old lady who seemed to have appeared from nowhere.   We explained the purpose of our visit, and she proceeded to show us round.   On the first floor were two rooms excellently furnished, but devoid of glass in the windows.   They had been occupied by our predecessors, but several shells dropping in the immediate vicinity had induced them to move elsewhere.   We considered their move to have been well advised, so, taking the wooden beds —with the old lady's permission—we left her once more to her solitude and lonely fears.

Whilst at Honnevain I made two expeditions into Froyennes.   The first time I went with another officer to see the nuns there.   We found them living in the cellars of their Convent, and apparently resigned and cheerful under the novel and trying conditions of life.   The second time I went up alone to see the South Lancs., and after lunch in the fine house which served as their Headquarters, we went to visit a

Countess, of great local fame among the troops, whose large modern Château was the Headquarters of one of the front line companies, and only about five minutes' walk from the front line posts. The cellars were occupied partly by soldiers, partly by refugees from the neighbourhood, but the Countess herself we found in rooms on the first floor. She came downstairs and greeted us most cordially, and told us several anecdotes of the German occupation, how Prince Rupprecht of Bavaria used to ride in her park, and had all the paths dug up to make soft going for his horses, how, in his dread of bombing —of which apparently the Germans were universally terrified—he kept one house in Tournai, and passed the night in another house outside the town, where the danger would be less She offered to receive us in her drawing-room, but remarked that it would probably be as cold there as in the hall where we were, since all the windows were broken. After a few minutes' conversation we said good-bye, and I made my way back to Honnevain, calling in on the way to see an English family, who had settled in Froyennes just before the war, and whose house was now serving as Headquarters for our Brigade Light Trench Mortar Battery.

That night at Honnevain we were rudely disturbed by a shell which dropped on the road outside our farm, broke the windows of the Adjutant's room to pieces, and very nearly hit that officer himself.

The next evening, 31st October, we were relieved by the 17th Londons in the 47th Division, and when all the Companies had moved back we at Headquarters got on our horses and rode back in the dark over hedges and ditches to " Hardy Planck " Farm, where the Battalion was assembling and having tea before marching away.   This was my last night ride back from the line ; the first had been from Foncque-villers to St Amand in October 1916 when I was with the Gloucesters, the second from Inchy to Bullecourt with the Doctor in September, and now this third and last one in October.

That night we marched to billets at Austaing, a village off the main Lille-Tournai road.   The following day, 1st November, we marched into Lille and were billeted in the Faubourg de Fives.   Ten days later the Armistice was signed.

EPILOGUE

THE preceding pages have dealt in the main with war as hard facts brought it home to me, but there dwell still in my mind, more abiding, perhaps, than these facts themselves, certain impressions gradually built up. If I think of the war as I knew it, I think of long, lonely rides which I took so often over great, wide, desolate, dreary spaces, made empty by men of all traces of man's ancient handiwork, except here and there an isolated grave or long disused cemetery, rides through ruined villages and untended fields and quiet woods. I think of the long marches, riding slowly, sleepily behind the weary columns; or again of what has been wittily but so truly spoken of as "the mud, blood, and boredom" of the Somme—a campaign that impressed me far more deeply than Ypres.

And then from inanimate scenes I turn to the men, whom one loved more than one could tell, and whose deaths were such deep-felt losses. How wonderful they always were, patient, plodding, so often soaked in rain, trudging from one cheerless abode to another, facing gaily the rising of each hopeless dawn, living out so often the brief months of a hard life, and cheerfully closing it in blood. Their language, which shocked so many, was as meaningless and harmless as it was too often filthy, and their very blasphemies were pathetic. I remember once, on a dark wet night in Archille Ravine on the Somme, passing a working party going up the line carrying duck-boards. There was the usual silence on the part of some and language from others, and as I knocked up in the darkness against one lad—I could no more distinguish him than he me—I heard him mutter to himself " and Jesus wept." What can one think of that? Not sheer blasphemy, but much rather the almost unconscious recollection of old words, remembered from long ago, and carrying to his own mind, now perhaps for the first time, a certain fitness for the present : a prayer though he did not know it. And then what conditions they so often lived in. A good billet was a barn with straw, that was luxury ; a bad billet, a bad line of trenches, no pen can describe, just as no mind can conceive, without having seen them, what such places could be like.

The officers—they were of course of all sorts— but how few and far between were the really unpleasant ones. One of the great joys of Army life was the welcome one might always expect from them. If one was stranded anywhere, or called in for a meal or for information at any Officers' Mess, one was always sure of a greeting. The Army was like some vast brotherhood : friendly hospitality one could meet with almost everywhere, and no matter what a man's belief or profession or antecedents, life in their company was almost wholly pleasant. Of course, in religious matters, the prevailing ignorance not simply of Catholicism, which one might expect, but of Christianity and religion in general, I can only describe as abysmal beyond all conception. Of course there were marked exceptions, but that was the general impression one got.

When the Munsters came to the Division the Irish question was one not unfrequently discussed, but I don't think I ever met in the Army a single Englishman, even amongst those most ready to lay down the law, who had even the remotest idea of Irish history, or of English history in its relation to Ireland, or who ever attempted to gain any insight at all into the Irish point of view, or to study the characteristics of the Irish people. Like religion it was not thought worth the while.

However, I would not close these few pages on a note antagonistic to those with whom I lived so long. Rather do I find all outweighed in the abiding remembrance of the pleasure of their company, without which life, so often otherwise hard and strange, would have been quite unbearable. With them, however, the most dismal of prospects would take on a rosy hue, and their laughter would mellow constantly the hard days and dark nights of the war.

PRINTED BY
OLIVER AND BOYD
EDINBURGH

SOME RECENT BOOKS

PUBLISHED BY

SANDS & CO.

VIA DOLOROSA
> A Novel. By "A North Country Curate." Cr. 8vo.
> Price 4s. 6d. net.

MYSTICS ALL
> By ENID DINNIS. Cr. 8vo. Price 4s. net.

GOD'S FAIRY TALES
> Stories of the Supernatural in Everyday Life. By ENID
> DINNIS. Cr. 8vo. Price 4s. net.

THE ONION PEELERS
> A Novel. By R. P. GARROLD. Cr. 8vo. Price 6s.

A MORE EXCELLENT WAY
> A Novel. By FELICIA CURTIS. Cr. 8vo. Price 6s.

O'LOGHLIN OF CLARE
> A Novel. By ROSA MULHOLLAND. Cr. 8vo. 3s. 6d. net.

THE RETURN OF MARY O'MURROUGH
> A Novel. By ROSA MULHOLLAND. Illustrated. Cr. 8vo.
> Price 4s. net.

NORAH OF WATERFORD
> A Novel By ROSA MULHOLLAND. Cr. 8vo. Price
> 3s. 6d. net.

SANDS & CO., LONDON AND EDINBURGH

THE TRAGEDY OF CHRIS

The Tale of a Dublin Flower-girl. By ROSA MULHOLLAND. Cr. 8vo. Price 3s. 6d. net.

THROUGH REFINING FIRES

A Novel. By MARIE HAULLMONT. Cr. 8vo. Price 3s. 6d. net.

THE MOTHER, AND OTHER STORIES

By P. H. PEARSE. Cr. 8vo. Price 2s. 6d. net.

WITH THE FRENCH RED CROSS

Tales founded on fact. By ALICE DEASE. Cr. 8vo. Price 2s. net.

A PARCEL FOR HEAVEN

A Christmas Book for Old and Young. By JEAN NESMY. Illustrated. Cr. 8vo. Price 2s. 6d. net.

DREAMS AND REALITIES

Poems. By ROSA MULHOLLAND Cr. 8vo. Price 5s. net.

MY BELOVED TO ME

Verses. By S. M. A. With Preface by the Rev. JOSEPH RICKABY, S.J. Price 1s. net.

THE STATION PLATFORM

And other Verses. By MARGARET MACKENZIE. Price 2s. 6d. net.

GREAT FRENCH SERMONS

(Bossuet, Bourdaloue, Massillon). Edited by the Rev. D. O'MAHONY, B.D. With an Introduction by Abbot CARROL, O.S.B. Cr. 8vo. Price 6s. net.

FIRST-FRUITS: MEDITATIONS

By Sister M. PHILIP (Bar Convent, York). Cloth, price 2s. 6d. net. Leather, 3s. 6d. net.

SANDS & CO., LONDON AND EDINBURGH

OUR LADY'S MONTH

Readings for May. By Sister M. PHILIP (Bar Convent, York). With a Preface by the BISHOP OF NORTHAMPTON. Cr. 8vo. Price 3s. 6d. net.

THE MOTHER OF PERPETUAL SUCCOUR

By the Rev. G. STEBBING, C.SS.R. Price 9d. net.

"WOMAN, WHY WEEPEST THOU?"

A Book of Comfort for those afflicted by the War. By the Rev. A. ROCHE With a Preface by the BISHOP OF BENTWOOD. Cr. 8vo. Price 2s. net.

CIVILISATION AND CULTURE

By the Rev. E. HULL, S.J. Cr. 8vo. Price 2s. net.

TRUE STORIES FOR FIRST COMMUNICANTS

By a Sister of NOTRE DAME. Illustrated by WILFRID PIPPET. Price 2s. 6d. net.

ST BERNARD

Vol. VIII. of the Notre Dame Lives of the Saints. Price 3s. 6d. net.

THE STORY OF THE CATHOLIC CHURCH

By the Rev. G. STEBBING, C.SS.R. Demy 8vo. Price 7s. 6d. net.

THE LIFE OF BLESSED MARGARET MARY ALACOQUE

By Sister M. PHILIP. With a Preface by the BISHOP OF LEEDS. Price 5s. net.

IN A MEDIÆVAL LIBRARY

Studies in pre-Reformation Literature. By GERTRUDE ROBINSON. Price 4s. net.

SANDS & CO., LONDON AND EDINBURGH